W9-AYR-812

EPILEPSY

—Diseases and People—

EPILEPSY

Mary Kay Carson

Enslow Publishers, Inc.

44 Fadem Road   PO Box 38
Box 699   Aldershot
Springfield, NJ 07081 Hants GU12 6BP
USA   UK

Library of Congress Cataloging-in-Publication Data

Carson, Mary Kay.
    Epilepsy / Mary Kay Carson
        p. cm. — (Diseases and people)
    Includes bibliographical references and index.
    Summary: Explores the topic of epilepsy, discussing its history, symptoms, diagnosis,
treatment, and possible ways to prevent some forms of the disease.
    ISBN 0-7660-1049-X
    1. Epilepsy—Juvenile literature. [1. Epilepsy.] I. Title. II. Series.
RC372.C37 1998
616.8'53—dc21   97-34160
                                                   CIP
                                                       AC

Printed in the United States of America

10 9 8 7 6 5 4 3 2

Illustration Credits: © Corel Corporation, pp. 12, 44, 57, 61, 77, 79, 80;
Cyberonics, Inc., p. 87; Giraudon/Art Resource, NY, pp. 21, 24; Mary Kay
Carson, p. 73; Robert J. Smith, Jr., p. 64; Siemens Medical Systems, Inc., pp. 47,
48, 50, 89; Wyeth-Ayerst Laboratories, p. 55.

Cover Illustration: William K. Geiger for National Institute of Neurological
Disorders and Stroke, National Institutes of Health

Contents

EPILEPSY

What is it? A physical condition that is caused by repeated and temporary electrochemical storms in the brain that briefly change how the brain works and result in seizures.

Who gets it? All ages, races, and both sexes. About one percent of the general population has epilepsy. About one hundred twenty-five thousand new cases of epilepsy are reported in the United States each year; at least one third are children.

How do you get it? The cause of most people's epilepsy is unknown. Head injuries, brain tumors, strokes, poisoning, and illnesses that cause infections in the brain are known causes. Some kinds of epilepsy can be inherited.

What are the symptoms? The symptoms of epilepsy are seizures. A seizure can involve losing consciousness; jerking muscles; staring; hearing, seeing, tasting, smelling, or feeling things that are not there; and sudden falls.

How is it treated? Seizures are controlled through prescription drugs, surgery, or sometimes a special diet.

How can it be prevented? Preventing head injury, illnesses that can damage the brain, and strokes can help prevent some kinds of epilepsy.

1

Electrochemical Storms in the Brain

One night at dinner, twelve-year-old Jennifer Lovell said her tongue felt tingly and weird—like she had just bitten it. The moment passed and no one thought much of it. At least not until a few mornings later when Jennifer's arms flew uncontrollably up into the air and her body began to jerk. Jennifer crashed to the floor, unconscious. It was as if an invisible giant had grabbed her, shaken her, and thrown her to the ground.[1]

Twelve-year-old Joakim Bergman sat on a doctor's examining table in his hometown of Stockholm, Sweden. He had been in this office a lot lately. So much so, that he and the doctor were on a first-name basis. Joakim called his doctor "Mia." Doctor Mia asked him to take a few deep breaths. In and out, in and out he breathed. Then all of a sudden Joakim

9

stared straight ahead with a blank look for a few seconds. Joakim did not see or hear anything during those seconds. Afterward, he could not remember what had happened.[2]

Who has epilepsy—Joakim or Jennifer? Jennifer does. Her jerking movements are called seizures. Having seizures and completely "passing out" or going unconscious is what most people think a seizure is like. Seizures like Jennifer's are called tonic-clonic seizures.

But Joakim has epilepsy, too. His "losing a few seconds" is just a different kind of seizure. It is called an absence seizure.

A seizure is an attack on the brain. These attacks cause the brain to not work right. A brain that is not functioning properly affects other parts of the body as well. Sometimes a seizure causes a person to fall over unconscious. Other times he or she might just "zone out" for a few seconds.

A seizure can happen to anyone whose brain is not working properly. It can be a one-time occurrence. But when someone has seizures again and again, it is called a seizure disorder, or epilepsy.

Epilepsy Defined

- Epilepsy is a chronic disorder of the brain resulting in the tendency to have recurrent seizures.
- Seizures are sudden, uncontrolled episodes of excessive electrochemical discharges of brain cells, which in turn, may cause changes in behavior, movement, or sensation.[3]

About 2 million Americans have epilepsy.[4] Many people with epilepsy are children or young adults. But older people have it too. Epilepsy happens to people of all ages all over the world.

Jennifer's and Joakim's seizures are not the only two kinds. There are at least twenty different types of seizures.[5] Many people do not even know they have epilepsy because their seizures are so faint—maybe only a tingling in the fingers for a few seconds. A person can have different kinds of seizures at different times. Joakim's seizure problems started with tonic-clonic seizures like Jennifer's. His absence seizures came later.[6]

Each person's epilepsy is different. Seizures are symptoms of epilepsy, like a cough is a symptom of a cold. Seizures can have many different causes. Often the cause is unknown. But what all seizures have in common are brain cells that sometimes malfunction and cause the brain to not work properly.

The brain and body communicate through electrochemical signals sent by nerves. A seizure happens when nerve cells in the brain suddenly start signaling too frequently. Normal nerve cells fire about eighty electrochemical signals a second. But during a seizure, nerve cells might fire as many as five hundred signals a second![7] That causes a "storm" of electrochemical signals. The brain cannot function correctly during these "electrochemical brainstorms." Whether a person falls down and convulses, loses a few seconds, or just gets a tingling feeling depends on where in the brain the overload happened and how far it spread.[8]

People with epilepsy play sports and have fun with friends just like everyone else.

Doctors diagnose epileptic seizures by talking to patients about what happens to them before, during, and after seizures. This information gives them clues to which kinds of seizures are happening. Doctors also check the brain to see how it is working or if it is damaged. This is a job for high-tech machines like EEGs (electroencephalographs) and CAT (computerized axial tomography) and MRI (magnetic resonance imaging) scanners.

Once doctors know the problem is seizures, most patients start taking prescription drugs. Most people with seizure disorders can control them with drugs.[9] Some people's seizures stop altogether after a few years, and they can stop taking medicine. But epilepsy is a chronic illness, which means it lasts for several years to a lifetime. Drugs do not work for everyone. Sometimes doctors will do an operation to take out the part of the brain that is damaged and causing problems. Other people—mostly children—have been helped by eating a special high-fat diet.[10]

People with epilepsy are often misunderstood. Epilepsy is a disease that has both physical and behavioral symptoms. Watching someone have a seizure can be very frightening, and it can look very strange. This has caused people throughout history to fear and push away epileptics. But people with epilepsy are not crazy, mentally retarded, or dangerous. They are just people who sometimes have seizures.

It is true that people who have epilepsy never know when or where they might have a seizure. This does not keep most people with epilepsy from leading normal lives. People with epilepsy control their seizures with medicines and go to work or school, have children, play basketball, and enjoy life just like everyone else.

2

Epilepsy Through the Ages

Epilepsy is as old as the human race. Prehistoric paintings inside caves suggest that even Stone Age people knew about seizures and tried to cure them.[1] Written accounts of epileptic-like seizures go back more than four thousand years. Around the year 2000 B.C. in what is now Iraq, an Akkadian medical text carved on a stone tablet describes a person having a seizure. It says that the person's neck turned left, the hands and feet were tense, and the eyes opened wide. Saliva foamed at the mouth, and the person lost consciousness.[2] People having seizures are also mentioned in ancient Egyptian, Babylonian, and Persian texts.[3]

In fact, epilepsy was probably around long before humans even existed. Animals have seizures too—cats, dogs, and cows can all have epilepsy. Their brains can malfunction with too many electrochemical signals, resulting in seizures. It seems that epilepsy is as old as brains are, just as car trouble is as old as cars.

The way people have explained epilepsy has changed throughout history. Many ancient peoples believed diseases came from gods or demons. But because epilepsy has both physical and behavioral symptoms, its sufferers were especially thought to be under the influence of supernatural forces.

The ancient Greeks thought that people having seizures were communicating with the gods. They called epilepsy the "sacred illness."[4] But not all Greeks thought this was true. After all, ancient Greece is where science first started. The ancient Greeks were some of the first people to look for and study real reasons for why things happened, instead of just blaming the gods.

One ancient Greek scientist was named Hippocrates. He is often called the father of medicine. Hippocrates wanted people to realize that epilepsy was just a disease, not something sent by the gods. So he wrote a book about epilepsy called *On the Sacred Disease* in about 400 B.C. In it, he said that epilepsy is not caused by the gods, but by a problem in the brain. He recommended that it be treated by diet and drugs.[5] Twenty-four hundred years ago, Hippocrates had already figured out that epilepsy is a problem in the brain that causes seizures. In fact, epilepsy comes from the Greek word *epilepsia*, which means "to seize."

The Dark Ages

Unfortunately, the ancient Greeks' knowledge of epilepsy seemed lost for thousands of years. During the Middle Ages in Europe, seizures were thought to come from demons or the devil. For example, a handbook on witch-hunting written by two Dominican friars in 1494 listed seizures as one of the ways to identify a witch. More than two hundred thousand women were tortured and killed by people following the instructions in this famous witch-hunting handbook, called the *Malleus Maleficarum* (Hammer of Sorceresses).[6] Some of those murdered were probably just women with epilepsy.

If people who had seizures were not thought to be possessed or to be witches, they were still feared and shunned. It was common to wrongly think that epilepsy is contagious, and many people were locked away in prisonlike hospitals for their entire lives. A common attempt at "curing" epilepsy during the Middle Ages was to make a religious journey to the house where Saint Valentine was buried in Germany. It is not known why this particular saint was thought to cure epilepsy. Perhaps it is because the word *fallen* in German sounds very much like the word *Valentine*.[7] Epilepsy was known at that time as the "falling sickness," since someone having a seizure falls to the ground unconscious.

Other medieval medical cures included eating ground-up skulls, burning the person's skull with hot iron rods, and cutting a hole into the person's skull in order to let out the "mischievous matter" causing the seizures.[8] Doctors of the time seemed to realize that epilepsy had something to do with the head or brain. But they did not know what the cause was or how to treat it.

Modern View of Epilepsy

Elizabeth Jackson lived in England in the mid-1800s. She was born with a condition that caused the blood vessels carrying blood to her brain to narrow. Sometimes her brain did not get enough blood, which brought on seizures. The kind of epilepsy Elizabeth Jackson had did not make her pass out or convulse during seizures. She experienced partial seizures, and would fall into what she called a "dreamy state" for a few minutes.[9]

In those days epilepsy was still very much a misunderstood disorder. People who had seizures were still being sent to live in insane asylums. Luckily for Elizabeth, her husband was one of the few doctors who actually understood what epilepsy was.

Her husband was John Hughlings Jackson. He was very devoted to his wife and to the quest to understand the disorder that troubled her. After Elizabeth Jackson died from a stroke caused by the same problem that brought on her seizures, her husband continued to have a place set for her at the dinner table. He ate alone at a dinner table set for two the remaining thirty-five years of his life after she died.[10] Hughlings Jackson, as he was called, also went on to discover a breakthrough in the cause of epileptic seizures.

John Hughlings Jackson was born in 1835 in the Yorkshire English countryside. As was the custom of the time, he apprenticed to a doctor as a teenager, then later went to medical school. He spent his forty-four-year career as a doctor at the National Hospital for the Relief and Cure of the Paralyzed and Epileptic in London. There he not only took care of patients with seizures, but also tried to determine what was happening inside their brains.

Jackson knew that not getting enough blood to the brain could cause seizures. This was his wife's problem. But he also knew that not everyone who had seizures had a lack of blood reaching the brain. What else could it be? What did all of the patients with seizures have in common? Jackson studied the brains of his patients after they died. During these autopsies, Jackson found that all of the brains had something in common—scars. Somewhere on each brain was an area with scarred tissue. Sometimes the brain scars had come from an injury to the head from a fall or an accident. Other times the scarring came from poison, tumors, or a lack of blood. It did not seem to matter what caused the scar. It was the scar itself that was linked to the seizures.[11]

Around the same time Jackson was studying seizures, other scientists were studying how the brain sent messages to the body along nerves. German scientists Gustav Fritsch and Edward Hitzig were finding through experiments that these brain messages seemed to be electrical. They made a dog move its legs by sending weak electrical currents to the front of its brain.

Jackson thought that the damaged cells in a brain scar could not "fire" or send their electrical messages correctly. Instead, they sometimes fired out of control, discharging electricity and causing a seizure. He wrote a now famous first modern definition of an epileptic seizure: "an occasional sudden, massive, rapid and local discharge of the gray matter."[12] Gray matter is brain tissue made of neurons, or brain cells.

The First Epilepsy Medication

It took many years for Jackson's correct theory that seizures were caused by electrical (electrochemical it was later discovered) misfirings in the brain to be accepted.

Meanwhile, epilepsy patients were still forced to live in mental hospitals through the early part of the 1900s. The public continued to be suspicious of seizure sufferers, though public opinion had changed from thinking that they were possessed by the devil to people with dangerous personality disorders.

During this time there was only one drug used to treat epilepsy. It was discovered in 1857 by an English doctor named Sir Charles Locock. The drug was a chemical mixture called bromide of potassium. It was a strong chemical, with some severe side effects that damage a person's general health. But it was the first drug that could help people control their seizures.[13]

An example of how a patient with epilepsy was treated during these times is the case of the famous Dutch painter Vincent van Gogh. When he was thirty-five years old, he was living and painting in the south of France. On Christmas Day in 1888, the police brought van Gogh to a doctor who diagnosed van Gogh's lifetime of "spells," where he cursed, sleepwalked, or undressed and then later did not remember a thing, as a form of epilepsy.[14]

Van Gogh was given bromide of potassium and was kept at the hospital. The drug helped van Gogh very little, and he continued to have seizures. Because they would not let him paint at the hospital, van Gogh moved to what was called an asylum for epileptics and the insane in the spring of 1889.[15] There he lived and painted some of his most famous paintings. Unfortunately, the story of van Gogh does not end happily. His seizures, as well as separate problems with mental illness, continued. The artist killed himself at the age of thirty-seven.

Epilepsy in the Twentieth Century

In 1912, a German doctor started treating his epilepsy patients with a drug called phenobarbital. It was a real turning point in the treatment of epilepsy. Phenobarbital stopped the seizures better than bromide of potassium, and without the poisonous side effects of bromide of potassium, the patients grew healthier and happier. By controlling seizures without making patients ill in other ways, phenobarbital finally began to chip away at the myth that people who suffered from seizures were mentally disturbed.

Another big step toward understanding epilepsy came in the 1930s with the invention of a machine called the electroencephalograph (EEG) by Hans Berger.[16] It reads and charts brain waves, the electrical patterns in the brain. Since seizures are caused when the brain's electrochemical impulses

This is a painting Vincent van Gogh painted of himself. Today his paintings are some of the most valuable in the world.

People With Epilepsy Through the Ages

Julius Caesar (100–44 B.C.) was one of the most famous Romans of all time. Caesar was a powerful general who became Rome's dictator.

George Frideric Handel (1685–1759) was a famous baroque composer. Handel was born in Germany but lived and wrote much of his most famous music in England. Handel is best known for *The Messiah*, an oratorio.

Napoleon Bonaparte (1769–1821) was one of the most brilliant military figures in history. He declared himself emperor of France in 1804.

Lewis Carroll (1832–1898) is the pen name of the English writer Charles Lutwidge Dodgson. He is most famous for writing *Alice's Adventures in Wonderland* (1865) and *Through the Looking Glass* (1872).

Alfred Nobel (1833–1896) was a Swedish chemist who invented dynamite. With the fortune his invention earned him, he established the Nobel Prize to help all of humanity.

Peter Ilich Tchaikovsky (1840–1893) was a Russian music composer famous for many operas, symphonies, and ballets. His ballet *The Nutcracker* is a Christmas favorite around the world.

Vincent van Gogh (1853–1890) was a Dutch painter. His paintings are some of the world's most famous and loved.

malfunction, an EEG pattern for a person having seizures usually looks different from that of a person without epilepsy. Now doctors had a tool to diagnose epilepsy. Newer and more sophisticated machines for looking at the brain and studying how it works have been invented since the EEG. But doctors still use the EEG in diagnosing epilepsy.

Newer and better drugs for controlling seizures continued to be developed in the mid-1900s. Between 1912 and 1974, eighteen different drugs were introduced for the treatment of epilepsy.[17] Today, there is a large variety of drugs for treating the many different types of seizures, and more are constantly being developed. Most cause some side effects, and not all work for everybody. But today, more than two thirds of seizure sufferers control their seizures with prescription drugs.

Operations have been performed on patients with seizures for thousands of years. Since the Stone Age, "doctors" have bored holes in the skulls of seizure sufferers in order to "free the demons" that were causing their seizures. This procedure was called trepanning. If the operation itself did not immediately kill the patient, a fatal infection often set in later.

Modern surgery for epilepsy started in the 1930s with Wilder Penfield, a brain surgeon who lived in Montreal, Canada. He performed surgery to remove brain tumors before developing modern surgeries for epilepsy. One of his first patients was his sister, Ruth. She had suffered seizures since childhood, and as she reached middle age, they worsened. Dr. Penfield believed the seizures were being caused by a brain tumor pushing on part of her brain. He convinced her that

Epilepsy did not keep Napoleon from becoming the emperor of France.

removing the tumor would get rid of the seizures, and he operated on her brain.

Though Penfield was correct about the tumor, he could not remove it all. Unfortunately, it had grown into parts of the brain too important to cut out. The tumor grew back and Ruth died within a year.[18] However, Wilder Penfield went on to do many brain surgeries and pioneered an operation to cure epilepsy called a lobectomy. In a lobectomy, a surgeon removes the scarred or damaged part of the brain that is causing the seizures. A lobectomy is only useful in epilepsy patients whose seizures come from a single removable area of the brain. It is only recommended if drugs have not worked, because it is risky. Patients can lose their memories, become paralyzed, or not be able to talk after brain surgery. But lobectomies have given many people seizure-free lives.

Knowledge about epilepsy has come a long way. Scientists and physicians have discovered some of its secrets. But the brain is a complex organ. It still holds many mysteries that scientists have yet to solve. Not all seizures are controlled by drugs, nor can their direct cause be pinned down. Research will surely bring more understanding of this complicated disorder.

Though most societies are more accepting of people with epilepsy today than in the past, misunderstanding, discrimination, and negative stereotypes still exist. Living with epilepsy continues to be a challenge.

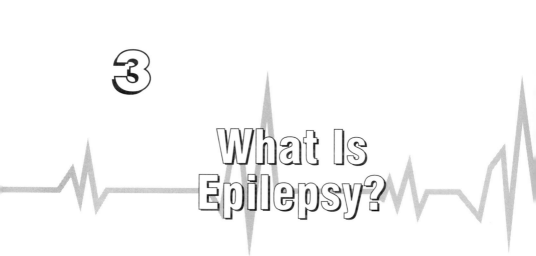

3

What Is Epilepsy?

I t was a sunny afternoon in late spring. Fifteen-year-old Tricia Nessler of Long Island, New York, was riding in the back of the Nessler's station wagon. Tricia, her friend Tracy, and the Nessler family were coming home from a trip to the country. Suddenly, Tracy started screaming to stop the car.

"It wasn't until we'd stopped and run around to the back that I saw that Tricia was unconscious," said Tricia's mom, Eileen Nessler. "The front of her T-shirt was covered with blood." Tricia's arms and legs thrashed and jerked with an eerie rhythm, her jaw clamped shut, and her eyes rolled back into her head. Tricia stopped seizing after a minute or two. Ten long minutes later, she finally regained consciousness.[1]

The Nesslers took Tricia to the emergency room of a nearby hospital. The doctor told the Nesslers that Tricia had had a seizure. He explained that it was not really as serious as it had looked. The seizure was caused by nerve cells improperly firing in her brain. But there would not be any permanent damage. Seizures do not usually cause brain damage unless they go on for a half hour or more. And all that blood? It was just from where she had bitten her tongue.

Everyone was relieved that Tricia was okay. But they were also worried. Could it happen again? The Nesslers wondered what was going on in their daughter's brain. They wondered if Tricia now had epilepsy.[2]

The Amazing Brain

The brain is an amazing and complex organ. You probably know that it is your brain that lets you think, do math problems, and talk. But the brain does a lot of other things without your ever "thinking" about them. Have you ever wondered how you "remember" to breathe when you are asleep, or how you can pull back your hand from a hot pan before you even realize it is hot? Your brain just automatically takes care of many body functions.

The brain is the body's command center. It processes and reacts to all the information coming from inside and outside the body. You need ears to pick up sounds. But it is not until after nerves in the ear have changed the sounds into nerve messages that the brain "hears" the school bell. And it all happens in a split second.

27

The brain as command center is broken down into many "offices," each with a specific job. For example, the area that controls vision is at the back, and the part of the brain for hearing is on the sides. Moving muscles and walking are controlled by the top part of the brain.

Neurons, Electrochemical Messengers

If the brain is the command center, the "wires" that carry and deliver its messages are the neurons. Neurons are the cells that make up nerves. Nerves are what sense temperature, light, sound, or pressure and carry messages in the body. Most neurons are too small to see without a microscope. Each neuron resembles a flower on a long stem with a few roots at the opposite end. Individual neurons line up "flower" end to "root" end to form loose chains and webs.

Neuron-filled nerves run from the spinal cord to the tips of your fingers and toes. When you touch a hot burner, nerves carry a message up the finger, through the hand and arm to the spinal cord. From the spinal cord, a message is sent along a nerve to the brain, which thinks "Hot!" At the same time, another message leaves the spinal cord to go back down to the finger, instructing your finger to get off the burner. The message to remove the finger is a split second faster than the one traveling to the brain, so you pull your finger back and then think "Hot!" Of course, it all happens much faster than you can read about it. The fastest neurons in the body carry messages at about 107 meters (350 feet) per second.[3] That is about 384 kilometers (240 miles) per hour!

The Brain Is the Body's Command Center

- The human brain has from 10 billion to 100 billion neurons, which transmit nerve impulses.
- Human beings have the most highly developed brain.
- The human brain is grayish-pink, has ridges and grooves on its surface, and weighs three pounds.
- The brain can go about three to five minutes without oxygen; after that, serious damage occurs.
- The brain has three main divisions: the cerebrum, the cerebellum, and the brain stem.

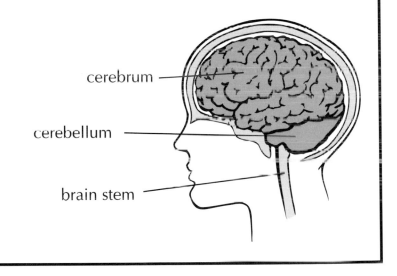

cerebrum

cerebellum

brain stem

Neurons are so speedy because the messages they send and receive are electrochemical. Electrochemical means chemical electricity. You know about a kind of chemical electricity—batteries. Batteries are filled with chemicals undergoing reactions that cause one end to have a positive (+) charge and the other end a negative (-) charge. This difference in charge is stored energy. By matching up the correct ends of the batteries in the radio, you release their stored energy to run the radio.

Neurons work in a similar way. Natural chemicals in the body cause each neuron to have a negative charge on the outside and a positive charge on the inside. Neurons have stored electrical energy, just like batteries. A signal or message travels down a neuron's long middle by releasing this electrical energy. This is a nerve impulse, or nerve "firing." Once the impulse reaches the end of the neuron it must cross over to the top of the next neuron. Special message chemicals called neurotransmitters are released into the area where the two neurons hook up. The neurotransmitter releases the next neuron's stored electrical energy and starts its nerve impulse—it fires it. This is how electrochemical signals and messages are passed along nerves to and from the brain and body.

Seizure Science

The brain is made up of billions and billions of neurons all connected into a complicated web that sends, receives, and processes messages. Your brain has more neurons than there are people on Earth! With all those neurons constantly working to keep everyone breathing, listening, hearing, feeling, and moving, it is no wonder that sometimes, in some people, something goes wrong. That something going wrong can cause a seizure.

Usually neurons fire in an orderly pattern. All the linked neurons in a chain must fire one after another in order to correctly pass along their message. But sometimes the neurons in an area of the brain do not fire in their regular orderly way. Perhaps they all fire at once instead of waiting their turn. Or maybe they fire too fast, as much as forty times faster than they should. These disorderly neurons can spread trouble to their neighboring neurons, spreading the "brain storm" all through the brain.

A person whose brain has neurons that are firing too fast or too often has a seizure. People who have seizures again and again have what is called a seizure disorder, or epilepsy. A seizure disorder is not a onetime illness like chickenpox. It is a chronic problem that may never go away, like allergies or asthma.

Causes of Epilepsy

Why do some people's brain neurons fire in a disorderly way again and again, causing seizure disorders? Neurons in the brain do not fire properly when they are damaged. Anything that damages neurons or causes neurons not to work correctly can bring on a seizure. Epilepsy has as many causes as there are ways that brain cells can be damaged. In many cases of epilepsy, the cause of the damage or problem is unknown. But some general causes are known.

31

Trauma—or injury—to the head can cause brain damage that leads to seizures. The head injury or brain cell damage could have happened during birth. Sometimes babies have a difficult time passing through the birth canal or do not get enough oxygen during birth. This can cause damage to brain cells. Falling and hitting your head, especially if you are unconscious for a half hour or more, can cause epilepsy. Motorcycle and car accidents also leave many people with head injuries. Dangerous sports like boxing, football, and rock climbing cause many head injuries each year as well. Head trauma is the known cause of the disorder in about a tenth of adults with epilepsy.

Brain tumors and diseases that cause infections and swelling in the brain, like encephalitis or meningitis, can also cause damage or problems that result in epilepsy. Peter, an eighteen-year-old high school junior, has seizures because part of his brain was scarred by an infection he had as a baby.

"I got sick when I was about six months old with what seemed like just a regular cold," Peter explains. "But it turned out that it was spinal meningitis (an infection in the lining of the membrane that covers the spinal cord and brain). I went into a coma for almost eight weeks. Ever since then, I've had seizures of one sort or another."[4]

Diseases and accidents are not the only known causes of epilepsy. Abusing drugs or alcohol and accidental poisonings can also damage the brain. The biggest known cause of epilepsy in elderly people is stroke. A stroke is when a blood vessel in the brain is blocked or breaks. Strokes often cause brain damage, which means seizures might follow. Stroke is the cause of epilepsy about one third of the time for people over sixty-four years of age.

Because so many cases of epilepsy have no known cause, many people mistakenly think it is always inherited. Inherited diseases, and inherited traits like brown eyes, are passed from parents to their children. A few kinds of epilepsy are inherited, though not many. Inherited epilepsy usually shows up in young children. About one fifth of the children under fifteen years old with epilepsy inherited it.[5]

Scientists have recently found a gene that causes a very serious kind of inherited epilepsy, called progressive myoclonus epilepsy. It is rare in the United States, but common in

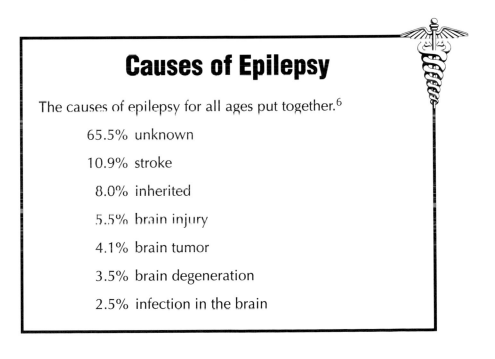

Causes of Epilepsy

The causes of epilepsy for all ages put together.[6]

 65.5% unknown

 10.9% stroke

  8.0% inherited

  5.5% brain injury

  4.1% brain tumor

  3.5% brain degeneration

  2.5% infection in the brain

Finland. The United States-Finnish team that discovered the gene does not know how it causes epilepsy yet. But if the team can figure it out, a treatment may be developed.[7] Scientists are working to find the genes that cause other kinds of inherited epilepsy as well.

When doctors do not know the cause of a person's epilepsy, it is called idiopathic epilepsy. *Idiopathic* is the medical term for "of unknown cause."

Types of Seizures

What happens to a person during a seizure? How long does it last? How serious is it? It depends on how many neurons are misfiring, and where those neurons are in the brain. If neurons in the part of the brain that controls hearing are not firing properly, for example, you might hear things or not be able to hear at all. What happens during a seizure depends on which brain neurons are not firing in an orderly way and what kind of seizure is happening. There are two main kinds of seizures: generalized and partial.

GENERALIZED SEIZURES

If the entire brain is involved in the seizure, it is a generalized seizure.

Tonic-Clonic Seizure. This kind of seizure is also called a grand mal seizure or a convulsion. It is often what people think of when they think of a seizure. It is very serious because it involves the whole brain and all the muscles, and because the person falls as he or she loses consciousness.

It is called tonic-clonic because it starts with a *tonic* phase, where the person's arms and legs stiffen and extend. Then it moves into a *clonic* phase, where the arms and legs jerk. A person having a tonic-clonic seizure loses consciousness, falls to the floor, stiffens, and begins to jerk as the muscles of the arms and legs tense and relax again and again. Sometimes people wet their pants, bite their tongue or cheek, or dribble a lot of foaming saliva. It is a myth that people having this kind of seizure will swallow their tongue.

The seizure usually lasts only a few minutes. As it ends, the jerking stops, the breathing becomes normal again, and the person regains consciousness. Often the person will be confused for a while, feel very tired, and possibly have a headache. He or she will not remember what happened during the seizure.

Juan, a seventeen-year-old who has had epilepsy for eleven years, describes a tonic-clonic seizure. "I never really know when it is coming. Suddenly, I black out. My arms and legs stiffen up, and my body jerks all over. I guess I bite my tongue sometimes, because there's often the taste of blood in my mouth when I wake up."[8] Juan does not remember what happens to him after he blacks out so other people report to him what happens. He just wakes up feeling tired afterward.

Jennifer, the girl who felt as if a giant had grabbed her and thrown her to the floor, and Tricia, who had had a seizure riding in the back of a car, were also both having generalized tonic-clonic seizures.

Absence Seizures. These seizures are also called petit mal. A person having an absence seizure "zones out" or "loses time" for a few seconds. One moment the person is alert, maybe talking or listening. And then the next moment he or she is staring into space unable to hear or answer. It usually passes in a few seconds, and the person returns right back to where he or she left off, totally unaware of what went on during those moments.

This type of seizure may not sound so bad. But a person might have as many as fifty of these a day. It is hard to pay attention in school or at work if you keep zoning out every half hour or so. Joakim, the Swedish boy, has absence seizures. They make it hard for him to pay attention in school.[9]

Sometimes a person has complex absence seizures. They are like the absence seizures just described except that the person may also blink rapidly, lightly smack the lips, or move an arm or the fingers a bit.

Absence seizures most often show up in children. Fortunately, about three quarters of those children stop having the seizures by the time they are eighteen.[10]

Atonic Seizures. These seizures are also called "drop" seizures or "drop attacks" because the person suddenly drops his head down. An atonic seizure causes a sudden loss of muscle strength. The eyelids shut, the head nods down, or he or she might even collapse. Consciousness might be lost for a moment, but often not at all. Some people who frequently have these kinds of seizures need to always wear helmets to protect their heads when they fall.

Myoclonic Seizures. During these seizures a person's muscles jerk for a short time. The neck, shoulders, upper arms, body, and upper legs jerk or jump by themselves. In children, these muscle jerks often happen right after they wake up in the morning. Sometimes a myoclonic seizure develops into convulsions. This kind of seizure is not usually outgrown.

PARTIAL SEIZURES

If only part of the brain is affected by neurons erratically firing, it is a partial—not generalized—seizure. Some people have a warning that a partial seizure is happening. The warning is something the person always hears, sees, tastes, or feels just as the brain starts having a seizure. This warning is called an aura and can be anything from smelling burned toast (that is not there) to hearing a ringing sound, or just having a "funny feeling."

Simple Partial Seizures. A person having a simple partial seizure does not lose consciousness or even "zone out." He or she is alert and awake, can answer questions, and will remember what happened during the seizure. What exactly happens during these kinds of seizures depends on the part of the brain affected. In some people, muscle control is affected and perhaps they stiffen, feel a tingling in an arm, or experience foot twitches.

Sensory control is another area of the brain that can be affected during partial seizures. Hallucinations, or hearing, seeing, smelling, tasting, or feeling things that are not there, is common. Feeling fear or other strong emotions for no reason also happens during these kinds of seizures. So is feeling as if you have already lived through this moment (déjà vu), are in a dream, or are not really yourself.

First Aid for Seizures

Not all seizures require first aid. These two kinds do.[11]

GENERALIZED TONIC-CLONIC SEIZURES

During the Seizure: The person may fall, stiffen, and make jerking movements. Pale or bluish complexion may result from difficult breathing.

- Help the person into a lying position and put something soft under the head.
- Remove glasses and loosen any tight clothing.
- Clear the area of hard or sharp objects.
- Do not force anything into the person's mouth.
- Do not try to restrain the person—you cannot stop the seizure.
- Turn the person on his or her side.

After the Seizure: The person will awaken confused and disoriented.

- Do not offer the person any food or drink until he or she is fully awake.
- Arrange for someone to stay nearby until the person is fully awake.

It is rarely necessary to call an ambulance unless:

- The person does not start breathing after the seizure (begin mouth-to-mouth resuscitation).
- The person has one seizure right after another.
- The person is injured.
- The person requests an ambulance.

(cont'd. on next page)

First Aid for Seizures

COMPLEX PARTIAL SEIZURES

During the Seizure: The person may have a glassy stare and not be able to answer simple questions. The person may sit, stand, or walk about aimlessly. The person may make lip-smacking or chewing motions, fidget with clothes, or appear to be drunk, drugged, or even psychotic.

- Do not try to stop or restrain the person.
- Try to remove harmful objects from the person's pathway or guide the person away from them.

After the Seizure: The person may be confused or disoriented after regaining consciousness and should not be left alone until fully alert.

As you can imagine, people with these kinds of seizures sometimes do not realize they are seizures at all. Many of these sensations are also symptoms of other disorders or problems.

Complex Partial Seizures. A person having a complex partial seizure does not lose consciousness and fall down, but the person is unaware of what is going on, cannot answer questions, and cannot remember what happened. During the seizure, a person may appear to be in a trance or sleepwalking. The person may walk around, mumble, or do things for no apparent reason. The seizure usually lasts just a few minutes, and the person may be confused and tired afterward. People tend to repeat the same behaviors each time they have a complex partial seizure.

What a person does during a complex partial seizure can seem quite odd. Mostly people just seem to "space out" for a while. But people have been known to take off their clothes, scream and yell, or pick their nose. Of course, these individuals have no memory of what they have done, nor can they control what they do during a seizure.

4

Diagnosing Epilepsy

One morning when I was about 14, while I was eating breakfast, my fork just flew out of my hand, sort of like someone grabbed it from me, taking my arm with it. My mom saw it happen. At first, we did not think anything of it, even when it happened again. But, a few weeks later, other stuff happened. I found that I would vomit whenever I got excited or sometimes for no reason at all. My mom decided to bring me to the hospital."[1] After describing what was happening to her and taking a number of medical tests, Lisa was diagnosed with epilepsy.

How can doctors tell when someone is having seizures and—more important—what kind of seizures they are? Just how does a doctor diagnose epilepsy?

Diagnosing epilepsy and deciding what kinds of seizures a patient is having are very important. The treatment given a seizure sufferer depends on an exact diagnosis. But it is not always easy. There is not an epilepsy germ that doctors can test for. Epilepsy is a disorder with a wide range of symptoms. Every case of epilepsy is unique.

Seizures are a symptom of epilepsy. But not everyone who has seizures has epilepsy. Having a high fever and taking some kinds of pills can bring on a seizure too. Panic attacks and other psychological problems can cause behavior that might look like partial seizures. In the past, someone who often fainted from low blood pressure might have been diagnosed with epilepsy. A student experiencing absence seizures might have been mistakenly labeled a slow learner.

Fortunately, medical specialists today are much better at diagnosing and treating epilepsy than ever before. Neurologists, or brain doctors, use a combination of modern medical tests and patient interviews to diagnose epilepsy.

Questions, Questions

A doctor who suspects a patient may be having seizures asks many questions. The doctor will want to know everything that happens before, during, and after the attacks to see if the events fit the pattern of any type of seizure.

The doctor will ask a variety of questions: How long do the attacks last? How often do they occur? What are you doing just before the attacks? Can you remember what happens during the attacks? Are you tired or confused after the attack? Do you get a headache? The person having the attacks might not know exactly what happens during the attack. Remember, many kinds of epileptic seizures leave the person unaware of what is happening or even unconscious. In this case, someone who has seen the person have the attacks needs to speak with the doctor.

Besides asking the patient to describe the attacks or seizures in as much detail as possible, the doctor will do a regular medical exam. The doctor will measure the patient's blood pressure and pulse, check the eyes and reflexes, and maybe test the blood or urine. The doctor must determine whether something besides epilepsy could be causing the problem. The doctor will ask the patient about the family's medical history, past accidents, other medical problems or sicknesses the patient has had, and whether or not any medication is being taken.

Catching Brain Waves

If after talking to and examining the patient the doctor suspects epilepsy, most patients will have one or more tests that look at what is going on in the brain.

Lisa, the girl who lost her fork at the breakfast table, had a number of tests done while at the hospital. She was given one test to measure the electrical impulses in her brain. It showed that some of Lisa's brain cells, or neurons, were firing erratically. That is what was causing her to vomit and her muscles to jerk.[2]

The test was an electroencephalogram (EEG). An EEG records brain waves—the brain's pattern of electrical activity or firing neurons. It can show if and where the brain's electrical

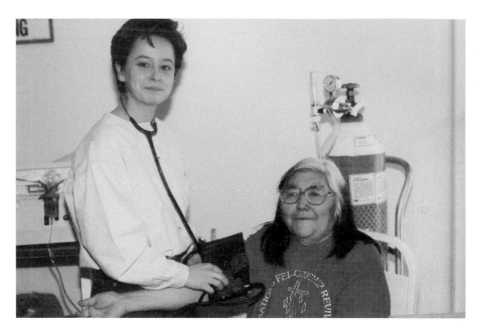

When a patient sees a doctor for seizures, he or she will receive a complete medical examination.

activity is not normal. It is commonly used to check for the unusual pattern of neuron firings that can cause seizures. It is the only test that can show actual electrical activity in the brain.

An EEG does not hurt and is safe. A patient sits in a chair or lies down. An EEG technologist pastes the ends of long thin wires called electrodes to different places on the person's head. The electrodes are shaped like small metal suction cups and go on the forehead, temples, and scalp. Since they can be stuck on through hair, no shaving is necessary. The other ends of the wires go into an electroencephalograph machine.

Once the patient is connected by electrodes to the machine, the machine is ready to record. The EEG usually records for at least half an hour. During that time, a line is drawn on a piece of paper for each electrode hookup. The lines make squiggly up-and-down marks as the EEG records the brain electricity passing under the electrodes. The lines are called traces.

Often the patient relaxes or naps while the EEG records. But sometimes the EEG technologist or a doctor wants to see how the brain reacts. The doctor may ask the patient to breathe in and out very quickly or may flash a light in the patient's eyes. These activities can trigger some kinds of seizures, which will show up on the EEG traces.

The doctor reads the EEG traces for signs of unusual brain activity. Regular brain activity shows lines with small hills and valleys. Neurons that are firing too often and too fast make EEG tracings with steep peaks and very low valleys. Not all kinds of epilepsy show up well on an EEG, but it is the most specific test doctors have.

Picturing the Brain

An EEG records brain activity, but it does not provide a picture of the brain itself. To actually see if and where a brain is damaged, doctors rely on other medical tests.

A CAT scan is a three-dimensional X ray. CAT stands for computerized axial tomography. During a CAT scan, a person lies on a table with a large circular machine around his or her head. The machine takes many hundreds of X rays at different angles. A computer puts them together into a three-dimensional (3-D) picture of the brain. Doctors can tell a lot by looking at a CAT scan. Scars on the brain, brain tumors, and blood all show up on a CAT scan. A CAT scan helps the doctor decide what may be causing the seizures and what treatment the patient needs.

If a clearer picture than a CAT scan is needed, a doctor does an MRI. MRI stands for magnetic resonance imaging. An MRI does the same thing as a CAT scan—it takes a 3-D picture of the brain. But an MRI does not use X rays. In a process similar to sonar, an MRI uses magnets and radio waves to map out images of the brain. MRIs are more detailed than CAT scans. If a small tumor shows up in a CAT scan, for instance, doctors might do an MRI to get a closer look at it. A patient getting an MRI also lies on a table with a large machine surrounding his or her head.

The newest way to look inside the brain is a PET scan. PET stands for positron emission tomography. It does not take a onetime picture of the brain like CAT and MRI scans do. It shows how the brain is working by observing it for minutes or hours.

A PET scan works by giving the patient an injection of glucose with a radioactive substance in it. Glucose is food for brain activity, and the radioactive substance is a marker or label—it is what the scanner will track and display. As the person's brain works and uses the labeled glucose, the scan shows the amount of food being used on a computer monitor. The outline of the brain will be displayed on the monitor with

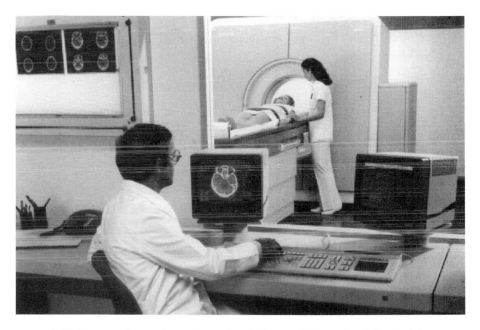

A CAT scan takes a three-dimensional X ray of the patient's brain. The image is shown on a computer screen.

47

An MRI scan uses magnets and radio waves to make a detailed picture of the inside of the body.

many different colors spread out in a number of areas. The colors tell the technician where the food is being used. While some colors mean a lot of food is being used—the brain is working hard—others mean little food is being used—there is little brain activity. By knowing which parts of the brain are working hard and which are not, doctors can look for tumors and other causes of seizures.

For example, an area of damaged brain cells will not use much food at all. This area could be where a patient's partial seizures are beginning. Pinpointing the exact area of seizures is especially important if the person is going to have brain surgery to stop seizures.

Scientists have used PET scans to learn the function of different areas of the brain. For example, scientists know what area of the brain is used while reading. A person having the scan reads and the scientists look at which parts of the brain are using the most food.

The Danger of Seizures

Diagnosing epilepsy can be difficult. No medical test is perfect and all patients are different. But by piecing together information from patients, parents, tests, and medical history, doctors try to solve the mystery of a person's seizures. Making the diagnosis of epilepsy is the first important step in getting the right kind of treatment so the patient can lead a more normal life.

Getting seizures under control is important to a person's health. Obviously no one wants to fall unconscious without a

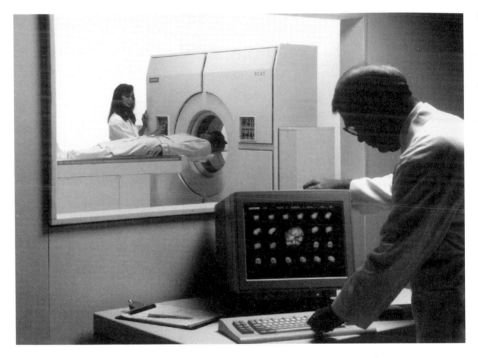

PET scans show how the brain is working, while it is working.

moment's notice, or "lose moments" throughout the day every day. Evidence also suggests that seizures are not good for the brain. Any one seizure does not cause brain damage. However, having frequent seizures may cause a person to have problems with memory—remembering everyday things can become more difficult. Scientists also think that improperly firing neurons could damage neighboring neurons. The damage could be spread this way, bringing on more seizures in the future.[3]

People rarely die from a single seizure. However, when a person has one seizure after another for more than about twenty minutes, death can occur. This is called status epilepticus. It can happen when someone suddenly stops taking epilepsy medication.[4] Immediate medical help is important because the person may not be breathing.

Regular seizures can make normal situations life-threatening, too. Someone having a tonic-clonic seizure while swimming could drown. Having any kind of seizure while driving can be dangerous for the driver and others on the road. Simply standing at the top of a flight of stairs could be dangerous for someone who has frequent seizures. These are all reasons why proper diagnosis and treatment are so important in managing epilepsy.

5

Treating Epilepsy

There is no cure for epilepsy. But many people with epilepsy live free of seizures. There is not any one best treatment for seizures. Because there are many different kinds of seizures and no two cases of epilepsy are the same, there are a number of treatments available. Not all treatments work for everybody, and for an unfortunate few, nothing works. But most people with epilepsy do find a treatment that controls their seizures.

Antiepileptic Drugs

Medications are by far the most common way people control their seizures. Herbs and other home remedies have been given to people with seizures for hundreds of years. The chemical potassium of bromide was given to people with seizures as early as 1857.

The modern era of treating seizures with drugs started in 1912 with phenobarbital. Phenobarbital is a sedative. Sedatives calm the body, and in the process keep some kinds of seizures from happening. But as anyone who has ever taken a sedative—like a sleeping pill—knows, sedatives can make you drowsy.

Today, there are more than twenty different epilepsy drugs available.[1] This wide variety of drugs allows patients and doctors to choose the medicines that work best for the individual person. The prescription depends on what kind of seizures the patient is having, how old the person is, what other drugs the person takes, and how that particular person's body reacts to and tolerates the drug.

Epilepsy drugs are strong medicines. Many cause some side effects. A side effect is what a drug does besides treat the disease it is prescribed for. For example, a side effect of aspirin for many people is an upset stomach.

Side effects from epilepsy medicines vary from drug to drug. They include rashes, gaining weight, feeling sick to the stomach, acne, and mood swings. Sedatives like phenobarbital not only can cause drowsiness, but can also cause memory loss.

"My memory stinks," says Jennifer Lovell who takes epilepsy drugs to prevent tonic-clonic seizures. "There are parts of my life—things I've done, films I've seen, books I've read, people I've met—that I cannot remember."[2]

How do epilepsy drugs stop seizures? The swallowed pills or liquid is digested in the small intestine. Then the drug's chemicals travel through the blood to the brain. It is not completely understood how the drug stops seizures once it is in the brain.

The brain is full of chemical messengers. Some of these messengers stop and start the firing of neurons in brain cells. Drugs used to treat epilepsy probably influence how these chemical messengers do their job. Some drugs seem to block chemical messengers that stimulate brain cells and set off seizures. Other drugs make the calming chemical messengers work harder, which can also prevent seizures. Still others might affect how the electrical charge of neurons is passed along a nerve.[3] Researchers are just not sure—there is much about the complex human brain that scientists do not understand.

Picking the Right Prescription

Getting the correct amount of the right medicine can be a challenge for many people with epilepsy. Doctors and patients work together—sometimes over months or even years—to find the best way to control the seizures. A patient might try a number of different drugs, change how much is taken, or even take a combination of drugs before finally getting the seizures under control. A doctor will test the patient's blood often during this trial-and-error period to check the level of drugs circulating through the body.

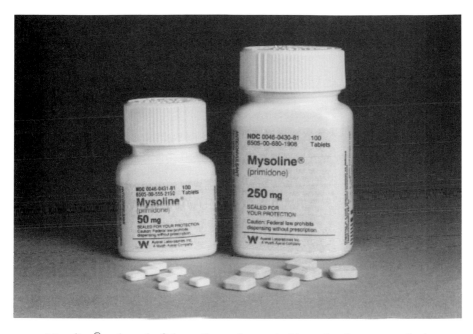

Mysoline®, a brand of the epilepsy drug primidone, has been prescribed since the 1950s to control seizures.

Once the best medication is found and the person's seizures are under control, regular visits to the doctor are still needed about every six months. During these visits the doctor will ask the patient about side effects and whether or not there have been any seizures. The doctor may check the level of drugs in the blood and do a regular physical exam to see if there are any problems.[4]

If someone with epilepsy stops having seizures over time, it might be possible for that person to stop taking medications. About half of the people who stop medication after their seizures have completely stopped for a number of years can eventually be seizure-free without their medications. It depends on the kind of epilepsy and the person. For example, many young people grow out of absence seizures.

Going off antiepileptic medication, however, can be dangerous. The amount of medication has to be lowered very gradually over many months. A patient cannot just stop taking epilepsy medications all at once—that could be very dangerous and may even cause serious seizures.[5]

Not all drugs work for all people. That is why the continual development of new epilepsy drugs is so important. A number of new epilepsy drugs came out in 1993, the first new antiepileptic drugs since 1977. One of these drugs, which came out in Canada, called vigabatrin, changed Michael Duffett's life. Duffett had suffered from serious seizures since childhood. As a ten-year-old in Newfoundland, he dreaded going to school. His thoughtless classmates teased him and called him "Fitso" because of his frequent seizures.[6]

Doctors tried all kinds of epilepsy drugs on Duffett, but nothing seemed to work. Between the seizures and the side effects of the drugs, it seemed as if Duffett would never leave home and become an independent person. But Duffett started taking vigabatrin at age twenty-three, and ever since, his seizures have stopped. "It has been my miracle," he said at age twenty-five. "Now, I can go where I want to, when I want to."[7]

These newest drugs generally have fewer side effects than the older ones, but they are still not perfect. Another of the promising new epilepsy drugs recently introduced was

Doctors must carefully weigh the seizure-controlling benefits of each antiepileptic drug with the side effects it causes when deciding what medication to prescribe.

Common Antiepileptic Drugs

These are some common antiepileptic drugs, the type of seizures they are commonly prescribed for, and some of their possible side effects.[8]

Drug Name (Brand Name)	Seizure Type	Possible Side Effects
CARBAMAZEPINE (Tegretol®)	Tonic-clonic, simple partial, and complex partial	Drowsiness, dizziness, nausea, blurred vision, headache, and blood disorders
CLONAZEPAM (Klonopin®)	Absence, atonic, and myoclonic	Drowsiness, dizziness, nausea, irritability, and changes in behavior
ETHOSUXIMIDE (Zarontin®)	Absence	Drowsiness, nausea, vomiting, and sleep problems
FELBAMATE (Felbatol®)	Partial, and partial that grow into generalized	Weight loss, headaches, liver problems, and blood disorders
GABAPENTIN* (Neurontin®)	Partial, and partial that grow into generalized	Dizziness, lack of coordination, and drowsiness
LAMOTRIGINE* (Lamictal®)	Partial, and partial that grow into generalized	Dizziness, lack of coordination, double vision, and rash
LORAZEPAM (Ativan®)	Repeating frequent seizures	Drowsiness, dizziness, irritability, and behavior changes
PHENOBARBITAL (Luminal®)	Most types	Drowsiness, irritability, dizziness, and loss of coordination
PHENYTOIN (Dilantin®)	Tonic-clonic, simple partial, and complex partial	Body hair growth, loss of coordination, gum overgrowth, blurry or double vision, and slurred speech
PRIMIDONE (Mysoline®)	Simple and complex partial	Drowsiness, depression, loss of coordination, and irritability
VALPROATE (Depakene® or Depakote®)	Absence and absence in combination with other types of seizures	Weight gain, hair loss, drowsiness, indigestion, nausea, tremor, and liver failure in young children

*Not yet FDA approved for children

felbamate. However, within two years of its release, fifteen people died from taking it.[9] It seems that the drug can be toxic to the liver and other organs and can cause the body to have problems making red blood cells. However, felbamate is the only drug that controls seizures for some people. Many of them choose to take it despite the risks. To them, being seizure-free is worth the risk.[10]

Surgery For Seizures

It all started with a car accident fifteen years ago. Fourteen-year-old Jennifer Claborn suffered some brain damage when she injured her head. It caused epilepsy. Her seizures were not too bad at first. About once a week she would have an unsettling dizzy spell. Claborn went on with her life, became a beautician, and got married. But while Claborn was pregnant with her second child, she started having serious convulsive seizures.

Claborn's seizures kept worsening over the next few years. Finally, her seizures were so frequent and strong that Claborn was unable to drive or care for her children alone. Claborn decided to have surgery. Doctors removed the damaged portion of her brain in what is called a temporal lobectomy. After the surgery Claborn completely recovered and has not had a single seizure.

"I'm doing everyday things and I love it," said Claborn. "My children have their mommy back."[11]

About one fifth, or 20 percent, of people with epilepsy who take drugs still continue to have seizures.[12] Some of them can benefit—like Jennifer Claborn did—from surgery. Surgery for epilepsy has come a long way in the past twenty-five years. New technologies like MRI and PET scans give doctors an inside view of the brain they did not have before.

Getting a good look at the brain is important. Epilepsy surgery is usually only helpful if doctors know exactly where the seizures are coming from. If doctors can locate the damaged area of the brain where neurons are not firing correctly, the person might benefit from having that area removed. Of course, the area causing problems has to be one a person can do without. Some parts of the brain can be removed with little effect, especially in younger patients, whose brains are still growing. But removing other parts of the brain can leave a person paralyzed or unable to speak, or could even erase a person's memory. Even a successful operation that removes problem-causing brain areas and stops seizures carries some risk of complications like problems with speech, memory, or muscle movement.

According to the Epilepsy Foundation of America, there are three main operations for epilepsy: lobectomies, corpus callostomies, and hemispherectomies. Each operation is different for different people, but all require opening up the skull during a long operation. A hospital stay of one to three weeks and then another month to two of recovery follow the operation.

Lobectomies are the most common operation for epilepsy. They are used for people who have partial seizures or partial seizures that turn into tonic-clonic seizures. The part of the brain that is causing the seizures is precisely identified and

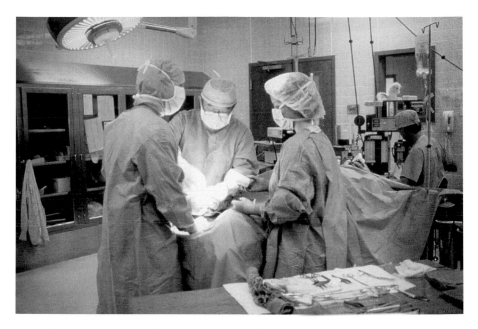

Stopping seizures with surgery is becoming more common as techniques and technology in the operating room improve.

located using CAT, MRI, or PET scans, or a special close-up EEG where the electrodes are placed inside the brain. Once the seizure-causing part of the brain is identified, it is removed in an operation.

Corpus callostomies can help some kinds of generalized seizures like atonic "drop" seizures. The corpus callosum is a bundle of nerve fibers that connects the two sides (hemispheres) of the brain and allows them to communicate. In a corpus callostomy, this connection is partially cut, preventing most seizures that start on one side of the brain from crossing over into the other side. No brain tissue is removed, and enough remaining connection is left for the brain halves to keep communicating. The person will still have seizures on one side of the brain—they just will not cross over to the other side.

Hemispherectomies remove most or all of one hemisphere or side of the brain where seizures are happening. These are done only in very severe cases, usually when the hemisphere is already very damaged and not functioning properly. The remaining half of the brain takes over all functions of the body, though the patient is usually left weak on one side of the body.[13]

Surgery for epilepsy is usually a last resort. It is only recommended for people with certain kinds of seizures that have not been helped with any medications. Brain surgery is always risky and there is no guarantee it will work. Many patients must still take medications after surgery to completely control their seizures. But surgery is a good choice for some people with seizures. A National Institutes of Health study found that between half and three quarters of patients undergoing epilepsy surgery were seizure-free after five years.[14]

Eating Seizures Away

Jim Abrahams is the producer of the movies *Airplane!* and *The Naked Gun*. One morning Abrahams's one-year-old son's head dropped and his right arm jerked straight up. Charlie was having a seizure. Soon he was having thirty to forty seizures a day. Even after trying different drugs and brain surgery, the seizures continued.

Finally, the Abrahams decided to try something entirely different. They took Charlie to Johns Hopkins Children's Center's Pediatric Epilepsy Center in Baltimore, Maryland. At the center, Dr. John Freeman took Charlie off the drugs and put him on a special very high-fat diet. Within a month, Charlie was seizure-free.[15]

This special diet is called the ketogenic diet. By eating mostly fat, a person's body makes many chemicals called ketones. A body with many ketones in the blood is in ketosis. Changing the body's chemistry so that it is in ketosis somehow helps to inhibit some people's seizures. Exactly how ketosis stops seizures is unknown, and not all doctors think it is healthy.

However, some epilepsy patients have had success with the diet, though many also take medications. It seems to work best in young children who have atonic, tonic, and myoclonic seizures that cannot be controlled with medications.[16] The ketogenic diet is very severe and can be dangerous. It is still an experimental treatment and needs to be further tested. A patient must start the diet in the hospital, under a doctor's care. For two or three days the patient eats nothing and only drinks a small amount of fluid. This starts the body going into ketosis. Then the patient starts eating high-fat meals.

A child on a ketogenic diet eats lots of cream, butter, mayonnaise, peanut butter, and other high-fat foods. He or she will also eat a bit of meat, cheese, or chicken, but not many carbohydrates like sugar, bread, and pasta. Some children cannot tolerate the diet. It makes them sick to their stomachs

Dr. John Freeman is a pediatric neurologist and the director of the Pediatric Epilepsy Center at Johns Hopkins Children's Center in Baltimore, Maryland. He is a supporter of the ketogenic diet.

and causes them to vomit. It is also low in vitamins, so most "keto kids" take vitamin supplements. A child has to be willing to cooperate, too. Cheating on the diet by eating something not allowed can lead to a seizure. Older children are often unwilling to give up pizza and cookies.

Children whose seizures are controlled by the diet might stay on it for a year or so. After that their doctor might slowly start to add more carbohydrates until they can eat like anybody else. Some children remain free of seizures after they are back to eating a more normal diet. In others, the seizures return, but drugs that did not control the seizures before will now do so.

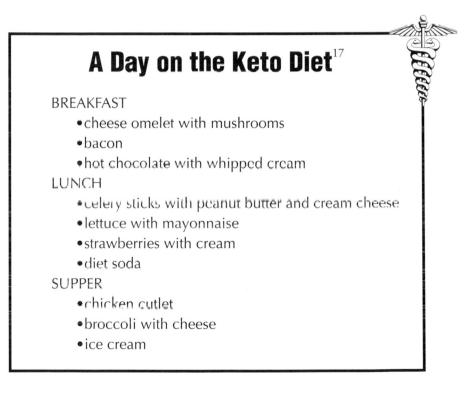

A Day on the Keto Diet[17]

BREAKFAST
- cheese omelet with mushrooms
- bacon
- hot chocolate with whipped cream

LUNCH
- celery sticks with peanut butter and cream cheese
- lettuce with mayonnaise
- strawberries with cream
- diet soda

SUPPER
- chicken cutlet
- broccoli with cheese
- ice cream

Other Treatment Alternatives

Epilepsy is a chronic disorder or disease. Many people live with seizures and the side effects of antiepileptic drugs for many years—or even for their whole lives. The goal of the majority of people with epilepsy is to manage their seizures and side effects as best they can. They try new treatments and learn how to best minimize their own seizures in addition to, or instead of, taking medications.

Too much stress can bring on seizures, according to some doctors and people with epilepsy. So reducing stress is a way some people help keep their seizures under control. Exercise, yoga, meditation, or other relaxation techniques—as well as getting enough sleep—can help reduce stress.

Biofeedback is a method of controlling the workings of the body that are usually automatic. For instance, a biofeedback computer might make a beep sound for every heartbeat. By listening to the beep and concentrating on making it go faster or slower, a person can learn to control how fast his or her heart beats. Some people with seizures have used biofeedback to learn to control their brain waves and reduce their seizures.

Some people with epilepsy have a "warning" that a seizure is about to happen. It can be anything from having a funny feeling or hearing a violin to smelling lemons. The warning is called an aura, and some people use it to stop the seizure from going any farther. Dr. Robert Efron was one of the first to teach patients to use their auras to ward off seizures. One of his patients always smelled a bad smell before a seizure. So he gave her a bottle of perfume to sniff whenever the aura happened. By sniffing the perfume when she had her aura, she learned to stop her seizures before they happened. Eventually all she had to do was think of the perfume's smell. Another person's aura was a tingling leg. By rubbing and scratching the leg when he felt it tingling, he was able to stop his seizures.[18]

"It takes less than a minute," says Alice Turner about the method she learned to stop a seizure. "One day I got out of bed real fast, and I got this suffocating feeling that takes away my vision (Alice's aura). So I deliberately made myself tense, and I used the tension to stop the seizure. I stopped it!"[19]

Every person is different, every brain is different, and so is every case of epilepsy. There is no one treatment that works for everyone. Every individual with seizures must work together with his or her doctor to find out what works best. It can take time and patience, but people with epilepsy can potentially gain a life free of seizures.

6
Coping With Epilepsy

When the pickup truck Tony Coelho was riding in flipped over, he got quite a bump on the head. Soon after the accident, the fifteen-year-old started having tonic-clonic seizures. Coelho's parents were children of religious Portuguese immigrants. They still believed the old superstitions that people with seizures were possessed by the devil. They took young Tony to exorcists, faith healers, and witch doctors who burned feathers and poured hot oil on him. The seizures continued, but no one told Tony he simply had epilepsy.

Tony Coelho did not find out what was wrong with him until he graduated from college in the 1960s. He wanted to be a priest, so he entered a Jesuit seminary. During a physical he learned from the doctor that epilepsy had caused his "fainting spells" all these years. He started taking medication and his seizures were successfully controlled.

"Now that it was understood that my repeated seizures resulted from a brain injury and could be treated, I thought everything would return to normal," said Coelho.[1]

But just the opposite happened—everything started going wrong. First, he was expelled from the seminary. Part of a 1917 church law said that, "those with epilepsy and those possessed by the devil could not be considered for ordination."[2] In other words, no one with epilepsy can be a priest. (The church rule was finally changed in 1983.)

Next, his driver's license was taken away, and his health insurance canceled. To make matters worse, no one would hire him when they found out he had epilepsy. "All of a sudden, all of the people who had wanted to hire me because I was an outstanding senior," said Coelho, "no longer had openings."[3] The Army, which was drafting men to send to the Vietnam War, would not even accept him.

Not much understanding came from his family either. When twenty-two-year-old Coelho told his parents he was diagnosed with epilepsy, they would not accept it. "No son of ours is an epileptic!" they said. They had known about his epilepsy all along, but had chosen to believe their son was "possessed." Coelho soon hit bottom, getting drunk every day and thinking about killing himself.

"I was out of work, out of luck and out of hope, scared to face the future in a world where no one wanted me," said Coelho. "I was an 'epileptic,' an outcast."

But with the help of friends, Tony Coelho pulled his life together. He started living with the entertainer Bob Hope and his family and doing odd jobs for them. Mr. Hope encouraged Coelho to find a way to make a difference outside of the church. "If you find your way blocked," Hope told Coelho, "find another route to get where you want to be."[4]

That "other route" turned out to be politics. Coelho started working for a local congressman. In 1978, Coelho was elected a Democratic congressman from California. Congressman Coelho did not forget what he had been through once he became successful. While in Congress, Coelho wrote the Americans with Disabilities Act (ADA). It says that no one can be discriminated against because of his or her disabilities. The ADA became a United States law in 1990.

"What I once considered a curse forced me to face life, shaped me and strengthened me. Above all, it gave me a mission as an advocate for people with disabilities," said Tony Coelho.[5]

Accepting Epilepsy

Carla Gray was in her twenties when she had her first tonic-clonic seizure. It happened while she was asleep. When she came to, her husband and dog were staring at her. Gray went to a doctor, was diagnosed with epilepsy, and started taking medication. But she admits that, "It took me a while to come around to the idea of having epilepsy."[6] After all, it was her husband who had been scared to death by her seizure. Gray herself did not remember a thing. After some time another night seizure sent Gray crashing to the floor, where she landed on her face. "It took that second episode and falling out of bed and getting a broken nose and two black eyes for me to really think this was serious," said Carla Gray.[7]

Accepting the fact that they have a serious problem can take many people diagnosed with epilepsy a while. Epilepsy is a difficult disorder to have. It is chronic, so it lasts for years or even a lifetime. People with epilepsy have to learn to live with seizures and the side effects of their medications.

"But do not let this thing run your life," recommended Carla Gray. She works and lives pretty much like she did before having seizures. And she has not had a seizure for three years now. But she takes her medication religiously. "It is like taking a vitamin. It is good for you, so you take it—everyday," said Gray.[8]

Getting epilepsy patients to take their medication regularly is sometimes tough. If they have not had a seizure for a while, some people think they do not need to take it. But Carla Gray and her husband, Randy Gray, compare not taking your medication to driving drunk—something bad will happen eventually.[9]

The Stigma Can Be Worse Than the Seizures

As if coping with seizures and the side effects of medications were not enough, a person with epilepsy must also deal with all the myths, fears, and prejudices about epilepsy. Epilepsy is different from many other diseases or disorders. Because it comes from a disturbance in brain electricity, seizures have both physical and behavioral symptoms. This has earned epilepsy a bad reputation as demon possession or mental illness throughout history. It has also labeled people who have seizures as crazy, retarded, or violent. Epilepsy has a stigma attached to it. Many people have a very negative view of epilepsy and of people who have seizures.

The belief that epilepsy means one is possessed by the devil is not very common anymore. However, many people still think that a person who has seizures is probably mentally retarded, mentally ill, dangerously violent, or unfit to hold a job. Fighting these negative attitudes about epilepsy can be harder for people with epilepsy than dealing with the disorder itself.

"A seizure is only a few seconds to a few minutes of a person's life," says Roberta Lindbeck, executive director of the Epilepsy Foundation for the Heart of America. "We do not think that those few moments should define a person."[10] She thinks calling a person an "epileptic" makes it sound as if having epilepsy is the most important thing about that person. It defines the person. Saying "a person with epilepsy" or "a person with a seizure disorder" tells it more like it is, according to the National Epilepsy Foundation. They and other organizations are working hard to try to change the public's negative attitudes about epilepsy.[11]

The Home Front

Ceily Turner's older sister, Alice, had frequent and uncontrollable seizures pretty much since she was born. Going to

Many organizations, including the Epilepsy Foundation of America, are trying to get the truth out about seizure disorders and epilepsy.

doctors, trying out new medications and treatments, and tutoring "Ali" to help her memory and schoolwork took a lot of her parents' time. This made fourteen-year-old Ceily feel jealous and ignored.

"I was so resentful of Ali," Ceily remembers. "When anything bad happened, I was to blame. Ali did not take the rap for anything! I was taken for granted, too. While my friends were grilled by their parents about where they had been, I was not even asked."[12]

Having a family member with epilepsy affects everyone. Brothers and sisters of children with epilepsy can feel jealous and angry about all the attention parents give the child with

Six Myths About Epilepsy

MYTH: Someone having a seizure might swallow his or her tongue and choke to death.

FACT: It is impossible to swallow your tongue. Forcing something into the mouth of someone having a seizure can be dangerous—you can break his or her teeth—and it is unnecessary.

MYTH: People with epilepsy cannot drive.

FACT: Most of the time a person with epilepsy can get a driver's license if he or she has been seizure-free for a time. How long depends on the state. It is usually three months to a year.

MYTH: Women with epilepsy cannot have children.

FACT: Most women with epilepsy can and do have perfectly normal children.

MYTH: People with epilepsy can become dangerously violent or crazy during seizures.

FACT: People with epilepsy are no more violent or crazy than the average person. Unfortunately, sometimes strange behavior during seizures is confused with mental illness or aggression.

MYTH: You can catch epilepsy from someone who has seizures.

FACT: Absolutely not. Epilepsy is no more contagious than a broken arm.

MYTH: Someone with a seizure disorder cannot hold a job.

FACT: The majority of people with epilepsy control their seizures with medications and can do nearly any job they are trained for.

epilepsy. Some epilepsy medications have the side effect of changing someone's personality or moods, which can be hard to understand and deal with. A child with a parent who has epilepsy can be very frightened at the sight of his or her mother or father having a seizure. A tonic-clonic seizure is scary and looks more serious than it is—especially if it is your parent.

Parents and children can help each other by talking about the seizures. Children will feel better if they feel free to ask questions about their own seizures, their parents' seizures, or their siblings' seizures. Epilepsy should not be a secret that no one ever talks about. Everyone needs to know what to do when the family member has a seizure.

Most cities have support groups for both people with epilepsy and family members of people with epilepsy. People can find comfort, understanding, support, and new ideas by sharing information and experiences in support groups. Family counselors can also help people cope.

Today, people with epilepsy fall in love and marry just like everyone else. It was not always so simple. Many states used to have laws forbidding people with epilepsy from marrying. Only in the last twenty-five years have Missouri and West Virginia changed their laws to allow people with epilepsy to marry.

Having children is also a part of the lives of many people with epilepsy. However, pregnancy is always a bit more complicated for women who take strong medications, including epilepsy drugs. Some—though not all—epilepsy medications can harm a growing baby inside the mother. This is especially true during the first few months of pregnancy when the baby's heart, liver, and other organs are forming.

Should a pregnant woman with epilepsy not take her medicine? Not necessarily. It depends on what kind of seizures she has and how frequently they happen. Having frequent tonic-clonic seizures is not good for a developing baby either. The baby could be injured during the fall or convulsions of a seizure. Oxygen can be cut off to the baby during a tonic-clonic seizure, too.

Women who have epilepsy and plan to become pregnant need to talk to their doctor. Together they can make some decisions about what is best for the woman and her future baby. For example, some women cut back on the amount of medicine they take during pregnancy. Others switch from taking two to three kinds of medicines to just one. Some women have gone off their medications altogether for the first three months, then started taking them again later in their pregnancy.

Most women with epilepsy have perfectly healthy babies. The chances of a woman with epilepsy having a baby with a major birth defect are 6 percent. The chances for a healthy woman without epilepsy are 2.5 percent.[13] Doctors are not sure why these mothers have a slightly higher risk.

Epilepsy at School

Kate Oswald is a nine-year-old fourth grader. Her seizures started a few years ago. They were so bad at first that she had to be hospitalized. Now, with medicine, they are under

Most women with epilepsy can and do have children.

control. But it has not been easy. One medicine she took for a while caused her to gain twenty pounds. And the medicine she now takes makes it hard for her to concentrate at school. Sometimes she takes tests out in the hall so she can think without distractions.

Kate is honest with people about her epilepsy. "It is important to tell my classmates, teachers, and coaches so they know what to do in case I have a seizure," Kate explained.[14] But after she told her class at the beginning of the year, some of the children called her "seizure kid." Classmates also stopped inviting her to parties and sleepovers. People were afraid she would have a seizure and they would not know what to do. Things got better after a while, but it still hurt. "I want people to know that just because I have seizures does not mean I'm not a regular kid. I want to be treated just like anybody else," said Kate.[15]

Every year about one hundred twenty-five thousand new cases of epilepsy are diagnosed in the United States. About half of those are children and adolescents.[16] It can cause problems for them at school. Some, like Kate, have trouble concentrating because of the medications they take to control seizures. Children with partial seizures might "zone out" during school a couple of times a day. This can also make it hard for them to keep up with what is going on in class. Other children with frequent partial seizures have been accused of taking illegal drugs. Of course, some children with epilepsy show no signs of having seizures or side effects at all. Remember, no two people's epilepsy is the same.

Teachers can help children who have trouble concentrating and remembering by giving them more time to take tests, reminding them often of assignments, and getting tutors for them if they need extra help. Children can help, too, by just being a friend and treating them like anyone else.

School is always hard for any child who is seen as different in any way. Many people, including teachers and students, do not understand epilepsy. People are often afraid of and make fun of what they do not understand. Only by educating people about epilepsy will the stigma someday disappear.

Some students with epilepsy may find it hard to concentrate because of the side effects of their medications. Studying in a quiet place without distractions can help.

Most children with epilepsy can play sports as well as other children.

Working With Epilepsy

People with epilepsy are painters, writers, movie stars, members of Congress, doctors, and Olympic athletes. Most people with epilepsy work, earn a living, and pay taxes like anyone else.

According to the Americans with Disabilities Act, it is against the law not to give someone a job he or she can do just because that person has a disability like epilepsy. Even so, many people with epilepsy have a hard time finding good jobs. Often when employers find out the person has seizures, someone else is chosen for the job. Even so, most people still say that honesty is the best policy when it comes to getting and keeping a job. People at work need to know what to do if you have a seizure.

Someone who has frequent tonic-clonic seizures probably will not get a job flying airplanes or working construction on top of skyscrapers. But neither would someone who is afraid of heights. Some people with epilepsy cannot drive, so that means delivery jobs are out of the question. But lots of people do not drive for many different reasons other than epilepsy.

Everyone has things he or she can do very well, as well as things he or she cannot do well or at all. People with epilepsy are good at some things and not others, too. Every case of epilepsy is different, and the abilities of each person are different. Workers with epilepsy have to match their skills and abilities to a job, just like anyone else.

"Know your limits. You know what you can do. You know what you cannot do," recommended Bob Paschall, a machinist

An Olympian With Epilepsy

French cyclist Marion Clignet used to ride for the United States team. But after the coach saw her having a seizure in an airport, he took her off the team. Luckily, the French team needed a fourth person to complete its team and chose Clignet.

Clignet has since led the French cycling team to victory many times. She has also finished in the top three in the Tour de France. Clignet's greatest victory came in 1996. She won the Olympic silver medal in the women's individual pursuit at the Olympic games in Atlanta, Georgia.

"If you want to do something, just go out there and do it," said Clignet. "Epilepsy is no excuse for not getting out there and pursuing your dreams."[17]

who has had epilepsy since childhood. He emphasizes keeping a positive attitude at work and turning people's questions about your epilepsy into a chance to teach them the truth about the disorder. After all, said Paschall, "Who's better qualified to educate someone about epilepsy than someone with epilepsy who's been there and done that?"[18]

7

A Future Without Epilepsy?

The United States Congress declared the 1990s the "decade of the brain." Researchers are discovering new ways of seeing, photographing, studying, and learning about the brain all the time. Scientists today know more about the brain than most once thought possible. But much about how the brain functions remains a mystery. There will be no cure for epilepsy until scientists know more about the brain and why seizures happen.

Research toward a cure for epilepsy continues around the world. Scientists are looking for the genes and hereditary causes of some kinds of seizures. Other researchers are studying all the different chemical messengers held inside our heads. New drugs and treatments could be developed by understanding how these chemicals relay messages to neurons.

While a cure for epilepsy will have to wait for the future, better tools for diagnosing epilepsy and better treatments for it are being developed today.

Newer EEG procedures can record both brain-wave patterns and a patient's behavior. A person spends a day or more hooked to an EEG while being videotaped at the same time. This gives doctors a better chance to catch unusual brain-wave patterns or seizures that might not happen during a regular thirty-minute EEG. When unusual brain waves are recorded, the doctors match them up to what the person was doing at the time they occurred by looking at the videotape. This can make hard-to-diagnose seizures easier to identify and treat correctly.

PET, CAT, and MRI scans are also getting more detailed and accurate. This will help doctors get a clearer picture of what a patient's brain looks like—and how it functions. The result should be a better understanding of what happens to a brain before, during, and after different kinds of seizures.

New drugs are constantly being developed and tested. And better tools for surgery, like lasers, will make for more promising and less risky operations.

Zapping Seizures

Chris Rich's seizures could not be controlled with drugs. So when a study of a new seizure treatment was announced, the twenty-nine-year-old volunteered. The study wanted to test if stimulating the vagus nerve could stop seizures.[1]

The vagus nerve is a major nerve that runs up the neck to the brain. Scientists think the vagus nerve is connected to parts of the brain where seizures start. Stimulating the vagus nerve with a little electricity may be able to disrupt the erratically firing brain cells enough to stop seizures. This is what the study wanted to find out.

Doctors implanted a small device the size of a pocket watch under the skin of Chris's upper-left chest. It has a tiny computer and a battery inside it. Wires from the device were snaked up through Chris's chest and attached to his vagus nerve. The operation took one to two hours, and Chris had to heal for two weeks afterward.[2]

Doctors program the device to send pulses of electricity up the wires to the vagus nerve. How often the pulses are sent, how strong they are, and how long the pulses last depend on what works to calm each patient's seizures. The patient and doctor work together to come up with the right combination.

The device's program is adjusted in the doctor's office, using a computer. Connected to the computer is a handheld programmer that the patient holds over his or her chest. The programmer "talks" to the device through the skin and sets the number of electric pulses per hour, their strength, and their frequency. This way, the doctor and patient can work together to program the device to best control seizures without having to reoperate.

Once the device is set, it sends pulses all day and night. (Some patients feel the pulses as a faint tingling, but others do not feel anything.) The device might be set to automatically send out thirty seconds of electrical pulses to the vagus nerve every ten minutes. But the patient can turn the device on and off with a small magnet. By holding the magnet over the chest where the device is implanted, the patient will switch it on. Some people try to stop a seizure they feel starting by holding the magnet over the device to switch it on.

Chris Rich had twenty-eight seizures during the three months before he had the device implanted. Three months after using the implant he had had only fourteen seizures. And all but three were quickly stopped with the device. He held the magnet over his chest when he felt the seizures coming on.[3]

Devices like these that stimulate the vagus nerve are still in the experimental stage. They are in the process of being approved by the Federal Drug Administration for the public. Someday soon it may be an option for those with seizure disorders who are not helped by medications or surgery.

Predicting Seizures

Knowing when a seizure is going to happen would be a big help to people with epilepsy. Some people get a warning or aura, but most do not. If you knew a seizure was coming, perhaps you could do something to prevent it—like take a drug or stimulate a nerve with the device described earlier. If you knew a seizure was on the way, at least you could get off your bike, sit down, pull your car over, or turn off the stove.

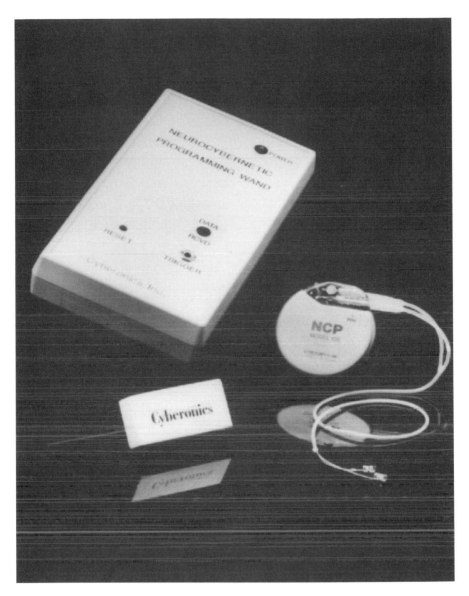

This is a device used for stimulating the vagus nerve, which stops seizures in some patients.

This would help in preventing accidents that might result from seizures.

Researchers are working on ways to predict seizures. One team at the University of Kansas Medical Center in Kansas City, Kansas, thinks it has found a way. Ivan Osorio and Mark Frei observed and videotaped epilepsy patients for days. At the same time, they recorded the patients' brain waves, using a video EEG. This way, they could see when seizures happened and know exactly what electrical activity was going on in the brain at the time.

Next, they took all this information and wrote a complicated mathematical problem or equation called an algorithm. The algorithm predicts a pattern in the brain waves. In other words, when the brain waves start to look a certain way, a seizure is almost surely on the way. A different algorithm has to be written for each patient, because everyone's pattern of seizures is different.

In experiments with patients at the hospital, the researchers have been able to predict the seizures about ten seconds before they happen. They hope to eventually be able to predict the seizures minutes in advance.

Obviously, no one is going to spend his or her life in the hospital, even if it means being able to know when a seizure will happen. People with epilepsy have lives to live, too! That is why the researchers are developing a wearable device that would warn patients. The researchers think that the best way to operate such a device would be to implant an electrode in the brain of epilepsy patients. The electrode would watch for

Better brain-imaging technology, like this detailed MRI scan, will continue to make diagnosing problems in the brain easier.

Can Dogs Predict Seizures?[4]

Christine Murray has seizures a few times a week. They leave her shaking uncontrollably for ten minutes or longer. She never knows when they are going to happen, but Annie does.

Annie is Murray's dog. She is a beagle and pit bull mix. A minute or two before Murray has a seizure, Annie jumps up into her lap and starts licking her face. Murray then knows it is time to stop what she is doing and lie down. A seizure is on the way.

How does Annie know that Murray is going to have a seizure? No one really knows. Some researchers think perhaps dogs can sense tiny changes in how the person is moving her muscles or how she smells right before a seizure.

There are many people with epilepsy who claim that their dogs warn them of seizures by barking or licking. Other dogs help their owners with epilepsy by making sure nothing is covering their mouth or by pushing their owner over on his side during a seizure.

"I never used to leave the house because I was afraid I'd hurt myself or people would think I was crazy if I suddenly had a seizure in a public place," said Christine Murray. Now she goes where she wants—with Annie along to warn her if a seizure is coming.

Annie's warnings have kept Christine from collapsing in the middle of a street and from falling down stairs. "Annie doesn't just warn me," said Murray. "She saves my life."

the pattern of brain activity that came before a seizure. When that pattern was detected, a message would be sent to some kind of wearable warning device that would buzz or beep, like a pager. The University of Kansas researchers hope to test their system soon.[5]

New Guidelines for Diagnosing Epilepsy

According to Dr. W. Allen Hauser, professor of neurology and public health at Columbia-Presbyterian, "There has been a debate in the medical community about how many seizures [usually occur before] a person should be treated for epilepsy." In February 1998, researchers announced new information that suggests that once a patient has a second seizure, the risk of having another seizure is high (73 percent) and a patient should therefore be treated for epilepsy after the second seizure.[6]

Prevention and Awareness

The cause of two thirds of the cases of epilepsy is unknown. But those cases caused by an injury to the brain often could have been prevented. In the future, better safety can reduce the number of people with seizures.

Car accidents leave many people with brain injuries that later lead to frequent seizures. Always wearing a seat belt, making sure small children are in safety seats, and having children sit in the backseat are all ways to prevent injuries and save lives. Wearing a helmet when riding your bike is another smart way to be safe and protect your head.

Preventing Brain Damage

Head injuries or other causes of brain damage can lead to seizures. Here are some things you can do to keep yourself safe.

- Always wear a helmet when riding a bike or motorcycle, in-line skating, playing football, skateboarding, kayaking, rock climbing, or doing any sport where you could hit your head.
- Always buckle up in the car—even if it is just a short ride. Sitting in the backseat is safest for children of all ages.
- Do not abuse drugs or alcohol.
- Eat right and get plenty of exercise to help prevent strokes when you are older.

Babies can be born with brain damage. A disease in the mother or a difficult birth can injure a baby's fragile brain. Mothers need good medical care during pregnancy and childbirth to help their babies be as healthy as possible. Heart disease that clogs arteries and causes strokes damages parts of the brain, too. Epilepsy in the elderly could be reduced as better stroke prevention and treatments are developed. Drug and alcohol abuse are also preventable causes of brain damage.

There is hope that someday, epilepsy will be a curable disorder. Many doctors and researchers are working to unlock the brain's secrets and solve the mysteries of epilepsy. Part of the battle is changing society's view of epilepsy and of people who have seizures. People who have seizures should not have to wait for the future to be thought of as the mothers, sons, lawyers, teachers, and friends they truly are, instead of as "epileptics."

Q & A

Q. Is epilepsy fatal?

A. It is extremely rare for a person to die of a seizure. For a person to die of a seizure, it would usually have to last for more than an hour. Fatal accidents do sometimes occur as a result of seizures, however. A person having a seizure while swimming could drown, for example.

Q. What causes a seizure?

A. Cells in the brain incorrectly sending electrochemical signals. The cells send too many signals too fast, which disrupts normal brain activity, causing a seizure.

Q. What should I do if someone is having a tonic-clonic seizure?

A. Help the person lie down, turn him on his side, and put something soft under his head. Move any sharp or hard objects out of the way. Do not try to put anything in his mouth. Stay with the person until he is fully awake.

Q. If someone has a seizure, should I call an ambulance?

A. It is rarely necessary to call an ambulance. Do not call an ambulance for a seizure unless the person does not start breathing after the seizure, the person is injured during the seizure, the seizure lasts more than twenty minutes, or if the person has one seizure right after another.

Q. What is an EEG?

A. An electroencephalogram. It is a medical test that records the brain's electrical activity, or brain waves. Doctors use it to look for unusual brain activity that could mean epilepsy. An EEG can also be an electroencephalograph, the machine that gives the test.

Q. Are people with epilepsy retarded or just crazy?

A. Neither. Epilepsy is not a mental illness or a learning disorder. It is a medical condition of the brain. Some people who are retarded also have epilepsy, just as some people who are retarded also have allergies. But having epilepsy does not mean the person is retarded or crazy.

Q. Do drugs cure epilepsy?

A. There is no cure for epilepsy. However, medications can help control seizures in most people.

Q. I know someone who started having seizures after being in a car accident. What can I do to help prevent epilepsy?

A. Protect and take care of your head! That means always wearing a helmet when biking, skating, or participating in dangerous sports like football, boxing, or rock climbing. Buckle up in the car. Do not abuse drugs or alcohol. Take care of yourself by eating right and exercising so you will not have a stroke later in life.

Q. Can people with epilepsy drive?

A. People with epilepsy who have been seizure-free for a time can get a driver's license. How long the person must be seizure free depends on the state. It is usually from a few months to a year.

Q. Do flashing lights and video games bring on seizures?

A. Not in most people with epilepsy. But some people have reflex epilepsy, which is triggered by flashing lights.

Q. My grandfather says epilepsy is a curse. Is he right?

A. Epilepsy is not a curse, possession by the devil, or a way to communicate with the supernatural. Because epilepsy affects the brain, it can have both behavioral and physical symptoms. This has caused a lot of fear and superstition about epilepsy for centuries. The truth is that epilepsy is a medical disorder like diabetes or asthma.

Epilepsy Timeline

2000 B.C.—Akkadian (present-day Iraq) doctors described a seizure in a medical text.

400 B.C.—Hippocrates wrote the first book on epilepsy called *On the Sacred Disease.*

1494 A handbook on witch-hunting written by two Dominican friars, called the *Malleus Maleficarum* (Hammer of Sorceresses), lists seizures as one of the ways to identify a witch.

1857—Sir Charles Locock reported the successful use of bromide of potassium in reducing seizures.

1873—John Hughlings Jackson correctly identified epilepsy as rapid and excessive electrical discharges of the brain tissue.

1891—The first hospital exclusively for people with epilepsy in the United States was established in Gallipolis, Ohio.

1912—Phenobarbital became the first modern antiepileptic drug.

1929—Hans Berger invented the electroencephalograph.

1930s—Wilder Penfield pioneered brain surgery for epilepsy.

1990—The Americans with Disabilities Act made it illegal to discriminate against people with disabilities, including epilepsy.

1993—Gabapentin, lamotrigine, and felbamate are
–1994 introduced. They were the first new epilepsy
drugs in fifteen years.

1996—A gene that causes progressive myoclonus
epilepsy, a rare form of epilepsy, was discovered
on chromosome 21.

For More Information

Epilepsy Foundation of
America
4351 Garden City Drive
Suite 406
Landover, MD 20785
1-800-EFA-1000
http://www.efa.org

Epilepsy Information Service
Medical Center Boulevard
Winston-Salem, NC 27157
1-800-642-0500

National Epilepsy Library
The Epilepsy Foundation of
America
4351 Garden City Drive
Landover, MD 20785
1-800-EFA-4050

National Information
Center for Children and
Youth with Disabilities
P.O. Box 1492
Washington, DC 20013
1-800-695-0285
http://www.aed.org/nichcy

National Institutes of Health
National Institute of
Neurological Disorders and
Stroke
Building 31, Room 8A06
Bethesda, MD 20892
(301) 496-5924
http://www.ninds.nih.gov

Chapter Notes

Chapter 1. Electrochemical Storms in the Brain

1. John Lovell and Jennifer Lovell, "I Am Not Defined By My Disorder," *Parade*, August 15, 1993, p. 6.

2. Thomas Bergman, *Moments That Disappear: Children Living With Epilepsy* (Milwaukee: Gareth Stevens Publishing, 1992), p. 11.

3. "Epilepsy: Medical Aspects," *Epilepsy Foundation of America* pamphlet (University of Minnesota, 1993), p. 1.

4. Shirl Rapport, "Hush, It's Epilepsy," *Newsweek*, August 1, 1994, p. 12.

5. Margie Patlak, "Controlling Epilepsy," *FDA Consumer*, May 1992, p. 30.

6. Bergman, p. 9.

7. Elaine Landau, *Epilepsy* (New York: Twenty-First Century Books, 1994), p. 12.

8. Steven Lewis, "Understanding Epilepsy," *Current Health 2*, December 1993, p. 20.

9. Patlak, p. 31.

10. Robin Sparkman and Geoffrey Cowley, "Can Fat Cure Epilepsy?" *Newsweek*, August 21, 1995, p. 56.

Chapter 2. Epilepsy Through the Ages

1. Roderick E. McGrew, *Encyclopedia of Medical History* (New York: McGraw-Hill Book Company, 1985), p. 112.

2. Kenneth F. Kiple, *The Cambridge World History of Human Disease* (Cambridge, U.K.: Cambridge University Press, 1993), p. 716.

3. Owsei Temkin, *The Falling Sickness: A History of Epilepsy From the Greeks to the Beginnings of Modern Neurology* (Baltimore: Johns Hopkins University Press, 1971), p. 7.

4. McGrew, p. 112.

5. Ibid., p. 8.

6. Orrin Devinsky, *A Guide to Understanding and Living With Epilepsy* (Philadelphia: F. A. Davis Company, 1994), p. 3.

7. Temkin, p. 101.

8. Tom McGowen, *Epilepsy* (New York: Franklin Watts, 1989), pp. 27–28.

9. Eve LaPlante, *Seized* (New York: HarperCollins, 1993), p. 11.

10. Ibid., pp. 11–12.

11. Ibid., pp. 13–14.

12. McGowen, p. 31.

13. McGrew, p. 113.

14. LaPlante, p. 5.

15. Ibid., p. 7.

16. McGrew, p. 114.

17. Ibid.

18. LaPlante, pp. 19–20.

Chapter 3. What Is Epilepsy?

1. Deborah Franklin, "The Case of the Star-Struck Teen," *Health*, March/April 1993, p. 40.

2. Ibid.

3. Orrin Devinsky, *A Guide to Understanding and Living With Epilepsy* (Philadelphia: F. A. Davis Company, 1994), p. 14.

4. Suzanne LeVert, *Teens Face to Face With Chronic Illness* (New York: Julian Messner, 1993), p. 43.

5. Devinsky, p. 44.

6. Ibid.

7 "Epilepsy Gene Identified," *Science News*, April 6, 1996, p. 221.

8. LeVert, p. 45.

9. Thomas Bergman, *Moments That Disappear: Children Living With Epilepsy* (Milwaukee: Gareth Stevens Publishing, 1992), p. 11.

10. Devinsky, p. 21.

11. "First Aid for Epilepsy," *Epilepsy Foundation Heart of America* card.

Chapter 4. Diagnosing Epilepsy

1. Suzanne LeVert, *Teens Face to Face With Chronic Illness* (New York: Julian Messner, 1993), p. 44.

2. Ibid., p. 45.

3. Margie Patlak, "Controlling Epilepsy," *FDA Consumer*, May 1992, p. 30.

4. "Epilepsy: Medical Aspects," *Epilepsy Foundation of America* pamphlet (University of Minnesota, 1993), p. 4.

Chapter 5. Treating Epilepsy

1. Steven Lewis, "Understanding Epilepsy," *Current Health 2*, December 1993, p. 21.

2. John Lovell and Jennifer Lovell, "I Am Not Defined By My Disorder," *Parade*, August 15, 1993, p. 6.

3. Margie Patlak, "Controlling Epilepsy," *FDA Consumer*, May 1992, p. 29.

4. James H. Fischer, "Making the Most of New Seizure Treatments," *Patient Care*, January 15, 1996, p. 60.

5. Ibid., p. 61.

6. Luke Fisher, "Prescription for Hope: New Drugs Can Help Many Epileptics Lead Normal Lives," *Maclean's*, July 10, 1995, p. 36.

7. Ibid.

8. "Properties of Commonly Used Antiepileptic Medications," Washington University School of Medicine card; "Epilepsy: Medical Aspects," *Epilepsy Foundation of America* pamphlet drug insert (University of Minnesota, 1993); "Drugs for Epilepsy," *The Medical Letter*, April 28, 1995, pp. 37–40.

9. Martin J. Brodie and John M. Pellock, "Taming the Brain Storms: Felbamate Updated," *The Lancet*, October 7, 1995, p. 918.

10. Ibid.

11. Ellen R. Seidman, "The Greatest Love of All," *Redbook*, May 1993, p. 192.

12. Jerome Engel, "Surgery for Seizures," *The Lancet*, March 7, 1996, p. 647.

13. "Epilepsy: You and Your Child," *Epilepsy Foundation of America* pamphlet, 1994, p. 17.

14. Patlak, p. 31.

15. Robin Sparkman and Geoffrey Cowley, "Can Fat Cure Epilepsy?" *Newsweek*, August 21, 1995, p. 56.

16. Orrin Devinsky, *A Guide to Understanding and Living With Epilepsy* (Philadelphia: F. A. Davis Company, 1994), p. 143.

17. Author's conversation with Dr. John Freeman, November 19, 1996.

18. Adrienne Richard and Joel Reiter, *Epilepsy: A New Approach* (New York: Prentice Hall Press, 1990), pp. 6–7.

19. Adrienne Richard, "Fighting for Alice: She Broke the Law to Give Her Daughter a Life," *Family Circle*, September 1, 1994, p. 83.

Chapter 6. Coping With Epilepsy

1. Tony Coelho, "Epilepsy Gave Me a Mission," *Exceptional Parent*, March 1995, p. 57.

2. Arthur Jones, "Why Tony Coelho Fights for the Disabled: Epilepsy Kept Him From Vietnam—and Jesuits," *National Catholic Reporter*, January 20, 1995, p. 3.

3. Ibid.

4. Coelho, p. 57.

5. Ibid., p. 58.

6. Carla Gray and Randy Gray, "Matrimony or Misery," *Open Your Mind to Epilepsy*, Epilepsy Foundation for the Heart of America symposium, November 16, 1996.

7. Ibid.

8. Ibid.

9. Ibid.

10. Roberta Lindbeck, "Responding to the Need," *Open Your Mind to Epilepsy*, Epilepsy Foundation for the Heart of America symposium, November 16, 1996.

11. Ibid.

12. Adrienne Richard, "Fighting for Alice: She Broke the Law to Give Her Daughter a Life," *Family Circle*, September 1, 1994, p. 84.

13. Orrin Devinsky, *A Guide to Understanding and Living With Epilepsy* (Philadelphia: F. A. Davis Company, 1994), p. 248.

14. Jayme Oswald and Kate Oswald, "A Family Coping With Epilepsy," *Open Your Mind to Epilepsy*, Epilepsy Foundation for the Heart of America symposium, November 16, 1996.

15. Ibid.

16. "Epilepsy," fact sheet, National Information Center for Children and Youth With Disabilities, FS6, August 1996.

17. "French Cyclist With Epilepsy Wins Silver Medal in Atlanta," *Epilepsy Foundation of America*, November 1996, <http://www.efa.org/newsdesk/news7.htm> (February 18, 1998).

18. Bob Paschall and Leland Reed, "Working With Epilepsy," *Open Your Mind to Epilepsy*, Epilepsy Foundation for the Heart of America symposium, November 16, 1996.

Chapter 7. A Future Without Epilepsy?

1. Donald C. Drake, "Implant for Epileptics," *Reader's Digest*, August 1992, p. 120.

2. Ibid.

3. Ibid.

4. Rajiv Chandrasekaran, "More Than a Best Friend," *Washington Post*, June 20, 1995, sec. B, p. 3.

5. Alan Bavley, "Researchers Predict Seizures of Epileptics," *Kansas City Star*, November 13, 1996, pp. A–1 and A–8.

6. Columbia University College of Physicians and Surgeons, "Researchers Establish Parameters in Epilepsy," *SciNews-MedNews*, February 12, 1998, <http://www.newswise.com/articles/eplpsy.cpm.html> (February 20, 1998).

Glossary

absence seizure—A whole-brain seizure where a person stares blankly or "zones out" for a few seconds and then later does not remember what happened.

atonic seizure—A whole-brain seizure where a person loses control of the muscles. The head often nods, a person drops what he or she is holding, and he or she might collapse and fall.

aura—A warning that a seizure is starting. It can be a feeling, a smell, or another sensation.

CAT scan—Computerized axial tomography. A computer picture of a three-dimensional X ray.

complex partial seizure—A part-brain seizure that does not cause loss of consciousness or collapse but the person unknowingly performs a complex behavior like mumbling or shuffling papers.

conscious—The state of knowing what is going on around you.

EEG—Electroencephalogram or electroencephalograph. The machine and test to measure electrical activity in the brain or brain waves.

epilepsy—A chronic disorder of the brain resulting in the tendency to have recurrent seizures.

generalized seizure—A seizure that occurs when the whole brain is overloaded by electrical activity.

generalized tonic seizure—A whole-brain seizure where the body stiffens.

generalized tonic-clonic seizure—A whole-brain seizure where the person becomes unconscious and falls, and the body stiffens and jerks. It used to be called a grand mal seizure or convulsion.

grand mal—An out-of-date term for tonic-clonic seizures.

hereditary—Passed on from parent to child through genes.

idiopathic—Medical term for "without a cause," meaning the cause is unknown.

MRI—Magnetic resonance imaging. A detailed picture of the inside of the body, created by magnets and a computer.

myoclonic seizure—A whole-brain seizure where the muscles jerk.

neurologist—A doctor who specializes in the nervous system—the brain, spinal cord, and nerves.

neuron—A nerve cell.

partial seizure—A seizure that occurs when only part of the brain is overloaded with electrical activity.

PET scan—Positron emission tomography. Creates a computerized picture of a working brain.

petit mal—An out-of-date term for absence seizures.

sedative—A drug that has a soothing, calming, or tranquilizing effect.

seizure—An activity caused by a brief change in how the brain works, due to a "storm" or discharge of electrical activity.

seizure disorder—Epilepsy.

side effect—A secondary and usually unwanted effect of a drug.

simple partial seizure—A part-brain seizure where a person does not lose consciousness but experiences repeated movements or senses things that do not exist.

status epilepticus—A seizure that does not stop. It can be either one long seizure or a series of repeated seizures. Emergency medical attention is needed, as it can be fatal.

stigma—A negative view, attitude, or stereotype.

unconscious—The state of not knowing what is going on around you.

Further Reading

Books

Bergman, Thomas. *Moments That Disappear: Children Living With Epilepsy.* Milwaukee: Gareth Stevens Publishing, 1992.

Devinsky, Orrin. *A Guide to Understanding and Living With Epilepsy.* Philadelphia: F. A. Davis Company, 1994.

Flanigan, Sara. *Alice.* New York: St. Martin's Press, 1988.

Freeman, John M., Eileen P. G. Vining, and Diana J. Pillas. *Seizures and Epilepsy in Childhood: A Guide for Parents.* Baltimore: Johns Hopkins University Press, 1990.

Landau, Elaine. *Epilepsy.* New York: Twenty First Century Books, 1994.

LeVert, Suzanne. *Teens Face to Face With Chronic Illness.* New York: Julian Messner, 1993.

McGowen, Tom. *Epilepsy.* New York: Franklin Watts, 1989.

Silverstein, Alvin, and Virginia B. Silverstein. *Epilepsy.* New York: HarperCollins, 1990.

Articles

Bavley, Alan. "Researchers Predict Seizures of Epileptics." *Kansas City Star,* November 13, 1996, pp. A–1 and A 8.

Brodie, Martin J., and John M. Pellock. "Taming the Brain Storms: Felbamate Updated." *The Lancet,* October 7, 1995, pp. 918–919.

Byers, Katharine. "One Day at a Time." *Exceptional Parent,* March 1995, pp. 19–21.

Chandrasekaran, Rajiv. "More Than a Best Friend." *Washington Post*, June 20, 1995, sec. B, p. 3.

Coelho, Tony. "Epilepsy Gave Me a Mission." *Exceptional Parent*, March 1995, pp. 57–58.

DeVore, Sheryl. "The Facts of Life With Epilepsy." *Current Health 2*, January 1989, pp. 10–12.

Drake, Donald C. "Implant for Epileptics." *Reader's Digest*, August 1992, p. 120.

Engel, Jerome. "Surgery for Seizures." *The Lancet*, March 7, 1996, pp. 647–652.

Fischer, James H. "Making the Most of New Seizure Treatments." *Patient Care*, January 15, 1996, pp. 53–66.

Fisher, Luke. "Prescription For Hope: New Drugs Can Help Many Epileptics Lead Normal Lives." *Maclean's*, July 10, 1995, p. 36.

Franklin, Deborah. "The Case of the Star-Struck Teen." *Health*, March/April 1993, pp. 40–42.

Gorman, Christine. "Taming the Brain Storms." *Time*, August 16, 1993, p. 42.

Jones, Arthur. "Why Tony Coelho Fights for the Disabled: Epilepsy Kept Him From Vietnam—and Jesuits." *National Catholic Reporter*, January 20, 1995, p. 3.

Lewis, Steven. "Understanding Epilepsy." *Current Health 2*, December 1993, pp. 19–21.

Lipsitz, Katherine H. "I Refused to Be Sick and It Almost Killed Me." *Mademoiselle*, April 1994, pp. 164–167.

Lovell, John, and Jennifer Lovell. "I Am Not Defined By My Disorder." *Parade*, August 15, 1993, p. 6.

Patlak, Margie. "Controlling Epilepsy." *FDA Consumer*, May 1992, pp. 28–31.

Rapport, Shirl. "Hush, It's Epilepsy." *Newsweek*, August 1, 1994, p. 12.

Richard, Adrienne. "Fighting for Alice: She Broke the Law to Give Her Daughter a Life." *Family Circle*, September 1, 1994, pp. 78–83.

Seidman, Ellen R. "The Greatest Love of All." *Redbook*, May 1993, p. 192.

Sparkman, Robin, and Geoffrey Cowley. "Can Fat Cure Epilepsy?" *Newsweek*, August 21, 1995, p. 56.

Index

M

Malleus Maleficarum, 16
medication. *See* antiepileptic
    drugs.
meditation, 66
memory, 40, 51, 53, 60, 73
meningitis, 32
MRI (magnetic resonance
    imaging), 12, 46, 60, 61, 84
myoclonic seizure, 36–37, 58, 63
Mysoline®, 58

N

Napoleon, 22
National Institutes of Health, 62
neurologist, 42
neuron, 19, 28–31, 34, 37, 43,
    45, 51, 54, 60, 83
Neurontin®, 58
neurotransmitter, 30
Nobel, Alfred, 22

O

Osorio, Ivan, 88

P

partial seizure, 17, 37, 39–40,
    42, 49, 58, 60, 78
Penfield, Wilder, 23, 25
PET (positron emission
    tomography) scan, 47, 49,
    60, 61, 84
petit mal, 35. *See also* absence
    seizure.
phenobarbital, 20, 53, 58
phenytoin, 58
pregnancy, 75–76, 93
primidone, 58

progressive myoclonus epilepsy,
    33–34

S

Saint Valentine, 16
sedative, 53
seizure disorder, 10, 12, 31, 72,
    74, 86
seizure types, 34–37, 39–40
simple partial seizure, 37, 39, 58
sleepwalking, 20, 39
status epilepticus, 51
stress, 66
stroke, 17, 32–33, 91, 93

T

Tchaikovsky, Peter Ilich, 22
Tegretol®, 58
tonic-clonic seizure, 10, 11,
    34–35, 38, 51, 53, 58, 60,
    68, 70, 75, 76, 81
tonic phase, 35

V

vagus nerve stimulation, 84–86
valproate, 58
van Gogh, Vincent, 19–20, 22
vigabatrin, 56

W

weight gain, 58, 77

X

X ray, 46

Y

yoga, 66

Z

Zarontin®, 58